LIFE LESSONS FROM THE MONASTERY

WISDOM ON LOVE, PRAYER, CALLING, AND COMMITMENT

JEROME KODELL, OSB

Cookie —

God bless you and your wonderful ministry

All + Jerome

Dec 5, 2013

the WORD among us® press

Published by The Word Among Us Press
7115 Guilford Drive, Suite 100
Frederick, MD 21704
www.wau.org

14 13 12 11 10   2 3 4 5 6

ISBN: 978-1-59325-166-6

Cover design by DesignWorks
Cover photograph: Saint Stephen's, Metéora, Thessaly, Greece

Made and printed in the United States of America

Library of Congress Cataloging-in-Publication Data

Kodell, Jerome.
Life lessons from the monastery : wisdom on love, prayer, calling, and commitment / Jerome Kodell.
    p. cm.
ISBN 978-1-59325-166-6
1. Christian life--Catholic authors. 2. Spiritual life--Catholic Church. I. Title.
BX2350.3.K63 2010
248.4'82--dc22
                                    2009037058

CONTENTS

INTRODUCTION

S everal years ago, I was surprised to receive in the mail from The Word Among Us Press a suggestion and a request for a book of short spiritual essays on the spiritual life. What caught my attention even more was the remark that I could draw on my nearly five decades of monastic life and almost twenty years as abbot.

Had it really been that long? It had, of course, and by now the "nearly" and "almost" are no longer necessary qualifications because I have passed both those milestones. Another implication of the suggestion was that *surely* I would have something to say after that much experience as a monk and abbot.

One thing that seems to have changed since I became abbot is that I have not attempted the book-length writing efforts I did before. All of my writing has become more limited in scope: conferences, homilies, retreat talks, letters, book reviews, articles. I had an idea of doing something more long-range at one time or another during recent years, but found that as abbot, I could not guarantee the stretches of writing time it takes me to sustain a larger project.

This has not been a handicap, since my office doesn't call for such lengthy productions. I have the time to do what I need to do. Most of my formal writing is in short commentaries, columns, or articles. A couple of times I have gathered together some of the individual articles for later publication. This is the first time I have written spiritual essays with the intention of publishing them as a group.

That doesn't mean these essays cohere tightly under an overall theme. They are simply a series of probes into the spiritual journey, as I have sought light here and there from ideas and experiences that have struck sparks in my mind along the way. Everyone's insight into the spiritual life is focused by his or her life experience, so it's no surprise that my meditations are mostly generated by monastic living and the reading of sacred Scripture.

But as I think about the origin of these essays, I am struck by how seldom they originated in a quiet time in my monastic cell. More often a train of thought was set off by interaction with other people, often outside the monastery, by a point that was made at a meeting, or by someone's comment on a news event or a Church development, or a question that stopped me in my mental tracks. It is a reminder about how much we all depend on one another, and how God speaks to us through others.

The implication of the invitation to write these essays is that I should have learned something from my experience over the years. If that is so, I think it has happened as it was described in the story of an old man, a famous guru, who was visited one day by a seeker. "O Wise One," the young man said, "how did you become so wise?" "Wisdom comes from good judgment," replied the guru. "And how did you get good judgment?" the questioner went on. "From experience," was the reply. "And how did you get experience?" he asked. "From bad judgment," said the old man.

Abbot Jerome Kodell, OSB

Part I

Divine Love
and Presence

1. "In Spite of" Love

In the opening words of his first encyclical, *God Is Love*, Pope Benedict XVI quotes words from the First Letter of John, which he says are a kind of summary of the Christian life: "We have come to know and to believe in the love God has for us" (4:16). Coming to believe in God's love, says the pope, describes the fundamental decision of our life (1).

This is not as easy as it sounds. There is love, and there is love. Someone has said that love is divided into three types: "because of" love, "if" love, and "in spite of" love. The first of these says something like "I love you because you are so beautiful" or "because you have done something for me." The second says, "I love you in the hope of what you can do for me or be for me." Many marriages are founded on one of these two types of love or a combination. These kinds of love are obviously very fragile and can fade when the circumstances change: you are no longer so beautiful, or you are not what I hoped you would be.

The third type of love says, "I love you for yourself, and this will not change in spite of what you do or don't do or whether you stay the same or become different." This is the only true love—unconditional love. The other kinds of love are only business deals.

When Scripture says, "God is love" (1 John 4:16), it means God is the third type of love, unconditional love. Psalm 56 says, "This I know, that God is for me" (verse 9, NRSV). God is totally for each of the children he has created. God does not love us because of what we have done, nor does he wait to love us until we do what he hopes. He does not withdraw his love when we disappoint him. He loves us completely, unconditionally, in spite of anything we might do.

The prophet Micah had his breath taken away by this vision of God: "Who is there like you, the God who removes guilt and pardons sin, . . . who . . . delights in clemency" (7:18). "Delights in clemency"—what a beautiful expression. God rejoices not in retribution but in mercy.

The pope says that coming to believe in God's unconditional love for us is what makes us Christian. It is much easier to believe in "because of" and "if" love, because they are all around us. We can understand acceptance and rejection, love given and love withdrawn, based on how we might look or act. But to believe in a love that is unaffected by anything we do or any characteristic we have requires that we move into a new realm of understanding.

Unconditional love expresses itself especially in undeserved forgiveness. "God proves his love for us in that while we were still sinners Christ died for us" (Romans 5:8). God did not wait for us to repent of our sins before he saved us through the death of his beloved son. And that is still true now: God loves us completely, even while we are in the act of sinning.

God sets the pattern for his children. The only way to achieve true peace and freedom is to learn to love unconditionally, "in spite of." "Blessed are the merciful" (Matthew 5:7)—Happy are those who, like God, delight in clemency. The school of love is a school of forgiveness, more precisely forgiveness of the inexcusable. There is a kind of forgiveness that comes into play when someone makes a mistake—misunderstands the time for an important meeting, or spills something on your shirt—but that is more excusing than forgiving. Real forgiveness can only take place when I have been hurt inexcusably. Yes, you lied about me, and that cost me my job. It is inexcusable, and you can't make it up. But I forgive you. This is unconditional forgiveness flowing from unconditional love, the kind of forgiveness we receive from God. Cardinal John Henry Newman called this "Christian revenge"—returning good for evil.

The act of forgiving lifts a great weight from the forgiver. It frees from the obligation to hang on to the hurt, and promotes interior joy and freedom. But vengeance makes more sense to our minds clouded by sin. And so it takes a great leap of faith to love one another as God loves us and to forgive as God forgives. We do not realize that forgiveness frees the forgiver even more than the offender, and that lack of forgiveness is a bitter trap. A Chinese proverb says that if you are going to take revenge, dig two graves.

This kind of love and this kind of forgiveness may seem too high and out of reach. That is probably because we equate love and forgiveness with feelings. It may be virtually impossible to feel forgiveness for someone who has harmed us purposely and inexcusably. We might do this once, but certainly not the seventy times seven times that Jesus expects. But the love and forgiveness required by the gospel are decisions. I love you when I want what is best for you and am ready to do what is best for you as much as I can. I don't have to like you. And what is best for you may be discipline, as with a child. I forgive you when I say in my heart, "I want to forgive you" or, if necessary, "I want to want to forgive you."

We are most like God when we love people who don't deserve it and forgive them when they do something inexcusable. That is what God does for us. And doing it for others is the best way we have of coming to know and to believe in the love God has for us.

2. HERE I AM!

Abeautiful Hebrew phrase appears at important times in the Old Testament: *Hineni,* Here I am! When God calls Abraham to sacrifice Isaac, Abraham answers, "*Hineni,* Here I am!" (Genesis 22:1, NRSV). I am ready to do whatever you say. Moses hears a voice calling from the burning bush: "Moses, Moses," and he answers immediately: "*Hineni,* Here I am!" (Exodus 3:4). Isaiah receives his prophetic calling in a vision in which God says: "Whom shall I send? Who will go for us?" Isaiah cries out: "*Hineni!* Send me!" (Isaiah 6:8).

This spontaneous response of a faithful disciple reechoes in the Bible, and it is wonderful and thrilling to hear. But even more wonderful is *Hineni* when God says it to us. Isaiah encourages us with these prophetic words: "You shall call, and the LORD will answer, / you shall cry for help, and he will say: *Hineni,* Here I am!" (Isaiah 58:9). I am ready to help you, God says, and I want to be with you. The same promise is voiced in Psalm 91, a standard part for centuries of the Compline prayer with which the Church sends us to bed: "All who call upon me I will answer; / I will be with them in distress" (verse 15).

What could be more comforting and consoling in my distress than to know that the God of the universe is with me? And not just "with me" in a dispassionate way, as an observer or a reporter, but as a parent who is engaged with me, cares for me, and loves me. When Moses was pleading his inability to be the leader of the people, God answered, "I will be with you" (Exodus 3:12). This was God's first answer to Moses (who asked a lot of questions), and it was the best answer that God could give or that Moses could hear. "I will be with you." But Moses couldn't hear it, at least at that moment. And for us, too, it is often hard to hear, but it is the best thing we could hear and the best thing God could say to us. "*Hineni,* Here I am!"

Here I am, wanting what is best for you and ready to do what is best for you. In Psalm 56, the psalmist cries out for help: "My foes treat me harshly all the day; / . . . All the day they foil my plans; / their every thought is of evil against me" (verses 3, 6). But because he knows the God he believes in, he is able to say, "O Most High, when I am afraid, / in you I place my trust. . . . This I know: God is on my side" (verses 3-4, 10). The last phrase is literally "I know that God is for me."

Hineni is a word we always need from God. The world is a dangerous place and human life is always precarious. We may reel under the realities of war and terrorism, be battered by financial concerns, family tragedy, personal sickness, or disability. The worst part of feeling besieged is feeling alone: I've got to bear this by myself. Parents may feel it at times in raising their children, or retired people when they see their savings evaporate, or those who are out of work, or who are lying in a sickbed or languishing in a nursing home. Here I am, alone. We may be bent over with the feeling that nobody can help us, and maybe, that nobody cares.

But God says to us: *Hineni!* Here I am. I am with you. Here is my Son. He loves you so much that he died for you. What an unexpected and glorious revelation! Not a distant God, but a God who cares, who loves us, who wants to be with us. When people are sick, suffering loss, experiencing tragedy, the best thing, the natural thing, is to go to be with them. Mary knew that Elizabeth had heard good news, but news that may have been overwhelming. She was reeling under her own news. She went immediately so they could be together. When Jesus was on the cross, Mary and the Beloved Disciple stayed under the cross. They could not save him, but they could be with him. Mother Teresa told her sisters: our gift to the dying is being with, not just doing for.

God does not say, "If you ask me, I am going to solve all your problems, make all your problems go away, make everything perfect." He does not say, "I will make earth heaven." Rather, he says, "I will be with you on earth so that you may open your heart to the desire for heaven and walk without fear, and so that you may share my love with others, saying to them in distress as I say to you: *Hineni,* here I am for you."

God gives himself to us in Jesus, and we give ourselves to one another. This is the meaning of the giving of gifts at Christmas: giving ourselves, our presence. Someone has said that the real meaning of Christmas is more often celebrated in our country now at Thanksgiving, when we don't have to worry about gifts. It is a time of just being together, which is the sharing of the greatest gift we have with one another. This is the gift God shares with us, his loving presence: I am with you in my son, Emmanuel. Be Emmanuel to one another.

The Emmanuel moment starts very early in our lives if we are blessed with parents who know how important their attitude of care is in delivering to their children the experience of God's personal love and care. In the middle of the night, we are wet and cold, and we wail for help. Almost immediately a loving presence is by our crib with a *Hineni* of soothing tones and touches. A playground collision or a collision of wills awakens in my small heart the fear that the world is a hostile, lonely place. But if someone is there to say, "Here I am," a spirit of fear and suspicion can be redeemed by hope.

We are sometimes convinced that all the news is bad, and that if we have hope, we are naïve. But the truth is that God is in the world, and because of that, every place is good. Poet Gerard Manley Hopkins reminds us that the world "is charged with the grandeur of God," and Cardinal John Henry Newman gives us this consoling thought: "In a dark world, Truth still makes way in spite of the darkness, passing from hand to hand" (*Parochial and Plain Sermons*, 1:22). God says to us continually, "*Hineni*, here I am, I love you," but he passes his message along through his children. We are the lifeline for one another.

3 · QUICK-EY'D LOVE

One day I was taking a leisurely stroll through the religious poetry in the back of the *Liturgy of the Hours* when a phrase from George Herbert's "Love" jumped out at me. The poem is an old favorite of mine, and you would have thought it didn't bear any more surprises for me. But that's the way it is with a classic. This time through, I finally noticed "quick-ey'd Love."

> Love bade me welcome; yet my soul drew back,
>   Guilty of dust and sin.
> But quick-ey'd Love, observing me grow slack
>   From my first entrance in,
> Drew nearer to me, sweetly questioning,
>   If I lack'd anything.
>
> "A guest," I answer'd, "worthy to be here";
>   Love said, "You shall be he."
> "I, the unkind, the ungrateful? Ah my dear,
>   I cannot look on thee."
> Love took my hand, and smiling did reply,
>   "Who made the eyes but I?"
>
> "Truth, Lord, but I have marr'd them; let my shame
>   Go where it does deserve."
> "And know you not," says Love, "who bore the blame?"
>   "My dear, then I will serve."

"You must sit down," says Love, "and taste my meat."
So I did sit and eat.

The host, of course, is God, welcoming the guest to a meal—
not just "Love" but "quick-ey'd Love," alert to every need and
concern of the guest before any needs are voiced. God notices
immediately the guest's uneasiness and feeling of unworthiness
in the presence of so great a host, and does everything to make
the guest feel at home.

Is there any description of true love better than "quick-ey'd,"
or any image of God more apt and appealing than "quick-ey'd
Love"? Think of a new mother with her baby, or an attentive
teacher with a slow student on the brink of blossom, or a nurse
helping an elderly patient in therapy. God the Lover's whole attention is taken up with the beloved, ready to serve at the slightest
indication of uncertainty, confusion, or need. There is no hanging
back, and certainly no hanging back in judgment, no keeping a
critical distance. God has his loving eyes on me at every moment,
ready to respond in a heartbeat.

"If God so loved us, we also must love one another" (1 John
4:11). We are all called to quick-ey'd love. This does not come
naturally to us. It requires God's grace. Our natural response is
quick-ey'd judgment. But we know that God is love, and whoever
remains in love remains in God. All Christian spirituality urges us
toward this love, but it is especially in the Eucharist that we renew
our covenant of quick-ey'd love. George Herbert was a dedicated
Anglican priest, and surely he appreciated the Eucharistic over-
tones in his poem. "'You must sit down,' says Love, 'and taste

my meat.' / So I did sit and eat." This meal nourishes us with the quick-ey'd love of God.

Besides being "quick-ey'd Love," God is also, to quote another poem, "The Hound of Heaven." And this vision of God reminded me of yet another image of God as the One searching for me and casting his loving eyes on me when he has found me.

All of us have been lost at one time or another, and we can relate to the feeling of being alone in a stalled car in a ditch on an icy night, on a remote country road miles away from help. The hours pass in waves of anguish or even terror. But suddenly a flashlight shines in your face, and you are looking up into the eyes of someone who loves you and has been searching for you ever since you didn't show up. At that moment of discovery, those are the most beautiful eyes in the world, the eyes of one who has been looking for me with love and has now found me.

God is the One who is always searching for me. God can always find me, because he is "quick-ey'd" and doesn't miss any of my moves. Maybe I am not always ready to be found. But any time I stop hiding my face and let God look into my eyes, God finds me. When I rest my gaze in God's, no matter what I call it, I am at prayer.

4 . PRESENCE OF GOD

Moses was frightened and daunted by the task God set out for him: to return to Egypt as an old man, to confront the authorities, and to lead the Hebrew people to a promised land. He questioned God about this choice, desperately trying to find a way to elude the mission. Right away God gave him the answer that is meant to calm all anxieties: "I will be with you" (Exodus 3:12). This answer is wonderful, but it is mysteriously very hard to hear, and if we hear it one day, it escapes us the next. But it is the answer to all our fears. And living by this truth is the mark of a person of faith. In the words of Cardinal John Henry Newman: "A true Christian may almost be defined as one who has a ruling sense of God's presence within him" (*Parochial and Plain Sermons*, 5:16)

The divine presence overshadows life in a Benedictine monastery. "We believe that the divine presence is everywhere and that in every place the eyes of the Lord are watching the good and the wicked" (*Rule of Benedict*, 19:1). Benedict goes on to say that there is one place where we are reminded of this in a special way: "Beyond the least doubt we should believe this to be especially true when we celebrate the divine office"(19:2). But the whole life is in God's presence. If we "yearn for life" and are ready to be converted to God's ways, "My eyes will be upon you and my ears will listen for your prayers; and even before you ask me, I will say to you: 'Here I am'" (*Rule*, Prologue, 18; Isaiah 58:9).

Benedict calls the monastery the "house of God," where God is incarnated everywhere: in the abbot, the sick, the guest, the old, the young. Even the tools used for work are to be treated as sacred vessels of the altar.

All of this is beside the point if the monk does not come to see that this presence of God is not merely institutional in some sense but is personal. God is with each one and in every detail of the day, "especially . . . in the divine office" (*Rule*, 19:2), but also at work, in private prayer, and in the daily interactions, which may cause frictions and even leave scars. God is taking care of each one personally.

This is true, of course, not just in the monastery, but anywhere people turn their lives over to God. Everything is seen in a different way if one has the "ruling sense of God's presence." But it is hard to realize in the middle of a stressful day when we are being pulled right and left.

When people visit monasteries, they often remark on the peacefulness of the atmosphere and say that they experience the presence of God. Sometimes the experience is even stronger for visitors who say they are not religious. Maybe it is a wake-up call for them. The monks are often amused when a guest says, "How peaceful it is here!" because it may not seem peaceful at all at that moment to those living in the monastery. Can't they see how we're running around, just trying to keep up?

The fact that those on the scene are surprised at the mention of peace may be the strongest sign of its presence. The peace of Christ is not the same as a superficial peace, which might be slow and tranquil on the surface but mask disorder underneath. The peace of Christ depends on the divine presence and is not something that can be manipulated or manufactured. But if it is present, it can be experienced no matter how busy the environment. And it will be present where people are seeking God, monastery or not. ✑

Part II

Prayer

5 . WE DON'T KNOW HOW TO PRAY

The words are so familiar that we hardly notice them as we hurry on to get to the main point. The main point is very powerful, but these are important too. And we would not be easily convinced that they are true except for the authority of the one who wrote them. The words are from St. Paul: "The Spirit too comes to the aid of our weakness; for we do not know how to pray as we ought" (Romans 8:26).

Paul goes on to explain that even if we can't express adequately what we want our prayer to say, the Spirit intercedes for us with "inexpressible groanings." God the Father, "the one who searches hearts," knows what the Spirit means, because the Spirit "intercedes for the holy ones according to God's will" (Romans 8:26, 27).

We all have anxieties about prayer: what formula to use, or to use no formula; how long and where to pray; what to pray for and whom to remember; to speak or be silent. St. Paul doesn't deny the importance of these concerns, but he tells us to put them in their place, which is a very minor place. It isn't our responsibility to pray perfectly. That would be an impossibility. He states flatly: "We don't know how to pray as we ought."

Think of what St. Paul is saying. All our worries about prayer are misplaced. The only thing that matters is to set aside time for prayer and to do the best we can. The Holy Spirit will take care of the rest. All we have to do is try. The Holy Spirit knows us better than we know ourselves. He reads our hearts, interprets our deepest desires, and takes them to the Father. As long as we try to pray, there is no flawed prayer and there is no fumble, no attempt at prayer that falls short. Every attempt at prayer is prayer because of the Holy Spirit's action on our behalf. This is an application of the overall promise in the verse just following the passage we have been quoting: "All things work for good for those who love God" (Romans 8:28). God wants to hear from us, and he doesn't care how feeble our effort. The Holy Spirit overrides any weakness and perfects our plea.

But this is just one side of prayer. Prayer is communication and communion. We think of prayer as something we do, but that is the smaller part. The greater part is the action of God. For God is praying in us even before we begin to pray. "The love of God has been poured out into our hearts through the holy Spirit that has been given to us" (Romans 5:5). When we pray, we dip into the eternal current of love that is in us by faith and grace. "It would not even occur to a person—nor to an angel or saint—to desire contemplative love were it not already alive with him" (*Cloud of Unknowing*, 34). Just as our communication to God is often beyond our expression, God's communication to us is often beyond our comprehension. When Mother Teresa was asked what she said to God when she stared silently at the tabernacle, she said, "I just listen." And what does God say to you? "He just listens."

Judging from the words of St. Paul, we can never expect to know how to pray, at least in terms of the knowledge we like to have. We can grow in prayer and become more and more at peace and confident of God's presence in our prayer, but we never will have a complete grasp of what is going on. This is not by accident. The control that knowledge gives would ruin our prayer. But when we come back day after day, often in the dark, we are forced to turn loose the control we love so much and throw ourselves on God. Our helplessness opens us to the grace of God's presence and deepens our faith.

God is not being coy by seeming distant. He wants union with us even more than we want union with him, and God is teaching us to pray as only he can. In his *Ladder of Divine Ascent*, written in the sixth century, St. John Climacus put it this way:

> God himself will teach you the art of prayer. We need no words to teach us how to see, for seeing is a natural faculty. Neither can we learn from others the beauty of prayer; its interior ways are made known to us by God alone, who gives to each the necessary knowledge and bestows the gift of prayer on those who pray. (28)

A baby is born with the equipment necessary for seeing and does not need instructions in seeing, even though he goes through stages until he is able to make full use of his eyes. We have the ability to pray but we don't know how. God will show us how to pray as we pray. Our part is to make the effort. Seven centuries after St. John Climacus wrote his words, *The Cloud of Unknowing* made the same point: "God is a jealous lover. He is at work in your spirit and will tolerate no meddlers. The only other one he needs is you" (2).

6. Two Minutes a Day

People are hungry for God. And God is eager to embrace people. Why is it that the search for God is often so difficult? Why do we flounder? Why is a personal experience of God so elusive?

I think the main reasons are these: (1) the language describing the experience of God is daunting and seems to put it out of reach; (2) we can't think anything so incredibly important can be simple; (3) when we do find a way of prayer that seems attractive and negotiable, we set the bar too high for ourselves.

All three of these obstacles are addressed in two sentences in *The Cloud of Unknowing*, the fourteenth-century spiritual classic. When you want to enter into the work of contemplation, "This is what you are to do: lift your heart up to the Lord, with a gentle stirring of love, desiring him for his own sake and not for his gifts. Center all your attention and desire on him and let this be the sole concern of your mind and heart" (3). Easy language, simple practice, accessible to all.

A word like "contemplation" can frighten us minor leaguers. How can I presume to contemplate when I hardly know the prayer ABCs? *The Cloud* makes it very simple: "Lift your heart to the Lord, desiring him for his own sake." No words, no thoughts, just a movement of love. Love here does not mean emotion. It means desire, an act of the will. Will I feel anything? Maybe so, maybe not. The experience of God is real, but it is on God's terms.

In our time, many people have come to discover the beauty of the contemplative experience of God in inspired movements like centering prayer and Christian meditation. These programs have broken through the mists, which had put contemplative prayer out of reach for ordinary persons, and retrieved simple prayer methods from earlier ages in the Church. The gift of personal experience of God in this way of prayer is transforming lives worldwide.

Ideally, in these methods a person spends two sessions of about twenty minutes each day entering into the divine presence at the beginning and end of the day in a beautiful rhythm. For most people, this is the pattern that is stabilizing and satisfying. But not for all. For some, it is too much, and they are afraid to attempt it or after a while cannot keep it up. Maybe this is a personal difficulty, maybe it is schedule pressure, maybe it is because of the busyness or distractedness of our age. But even this small requirement may put prayer out of reach for some.

The Cloud does not say anything about a length of time. It just calls for "a gentle stirring of love," which may take only an instant. The important thing is to come into God's presence daily, focusing on God for God's sake alone and bowing down in our hearts, recognizing who God is and who we are. Some may not be able to set aside longer periods of time for one reason or another. But everyone can come into God's presence daily to reach out in desire, and at least in a brief moment, to reestablish the relationship of child to Father and to open up to the transforming action of God's love. A longer time is always good, but just two minutes a day, if every day, is sufficient. It has to be every day, rain or shine, busy or free, happy or sad.

God needs only this tiny opening, just a crevice in the heart, to begin making a saint.

Once this brief humble turning to God makes it way into our daily schedule, we may find that our desire expands, and we are not satisfied with only two minutes. But two minutes is where many of us have to start, with no pressure for a large commitment and no fear of failure. The large commitment has been made by God, who desires us and is just waiting for us to come into the stream of his love. All it takes is "a naked intent toward God in the depths of your being" (*Cloud*, 3).

Every day the first hour of the Divine Office begins with an invitatory psalm that is a call to prayer. For centuries this was always Psalm 95, which contains these verses: "Come in; let us bow and bend low; / let us kneel before the God who made us / for he is our God" (see verses 6-7). At these words the monks would genuflect, beginning the day by expressing with their bodies the worship in their hearts. This is what we all must do interiorly, laying ourselves down in adoration every day, making ourselves available to God's transforming love. ∽∽

7. VACARE DEO

A favorite psalm verse for those who have awakened to the call of prayer is "Be still and know that I am God!" (Psalm 46:10, NRSV). This text has the power to calm us down, probably because it doesn't only call for silence but gives a reason, the best reason in the world, to "know that I am God," which translates as an invitation to come into communion with God personally and intimately.

The Latin form of this text is still familiar to older priests and religious, who until the mid-1960s prayed it in the Divine Office as *Vacate et videte, quoniam ego sum Deus*. It is not immediately obvious why *vacate*, which means in English "empty out," would be translated "be still," nor why *videte*, which means "see," would be translated "know." But these are faithful translations of the Latin (and of the Hebrew from which St. Jerome worked). In any translation from one language to another, however, the word in the original may have rich associations that cannot all be transferred to a single new word or phrase.

This is certainly the case with the phrase "Be still" in the psalm verse. In the spiritual tradition from the early monastic teachers, the injunction was *vacare Deo*, which meant more than simply being silent. It suggested making oneself "free for God," in the sense of emptying out any other preoccupations or interests when coming into God's presence. Our word "vacation" comes from this Latin root, and in a sense the psalm is calling us to "take a vacation with God"—not simply to be silent, but to be free to give all one's attention to God and relax in his presence.

To "be free for God" or "take time for God" adds a personal dimension. It is not merely a matter of being silent in awe of God—as "Be still, and know that I am God" might imply—but there is a sense of doing something with God in a familiar way, like "wasting time with God." This gives a sense of what St. Benedict intended for his monks in the ancient spiritual practice of *lectio divina* (divine or holy reading). He uses the verb *vacare* six times in the chapter of his *Rule* devoted to this practice. The translations have him encouraging the monks to "devote themselves to," "be free for" *lectio*. *Lectio* is a time to meet God in his holy word. It involves a range of practices centered on the biblical text, from word association to light study to contemplation, but it is not to be drudgery. It must be light, a time celebrating friendship with God through his word. Take a vacation with God.

The spiritual tradition of *vacare Deo* deserves a rebirth today, when people are strapped with work and trying to do ten things at once. We don't have much time for prayer, but when we do make time, we carry to prayer the same attitude we had at work: don't waste time, get the job done. We tend to be very businesslike. We know exactly what prayers we are going to say when we get on our knees, and when we're finished, we know whether or not we've succeeded in performing the program we assigned ourselves. There is pressure to do it right, but when we look more closely, we discover the pressure is self-imposed. Certainly the pressure to pray that way is not from God, who tells us—for he is the speaker in the psalm—to be still, but even more, to free ourselves to spend time with him. He is not freeing us from one rat race to bind us to another.

We will not be able to "take a vacation with God" simply by putting it on the schedule any more than we can "be still" at the flip of a mental switch. For many of us, *vacare Deo* may require a change in the way we think about our prayer. Prayer is neither a job nor an assignment nor a task. There isn't a USDA daily required amount. But until we set a daily time to be with God, we will not learn how to relax with him. When we see acquaintances only randomly, even if they are good friends, we must go through a certain ritual before we can relax together. In a way, we have to start over each time. It is the same in our time with God. As long as our visits with God are random or haphazard, we will not be able to have the kind of relationship with him that *vacare Deo* implies.

If our visits with God are random, they are probably driven by intermittent needs in our lives rather than a desire for relationship. We come like a niece or nephew hoping for a loan or gift from a rich uncle, something to tide us over until the next time. But when we start spending time with God every day, we realize that he has already been with us every day and knows us and our every need already. Even so, God wants us to tell him our needs and our deepest desires, because that will help us become free in his presence. But most of all, he wants us to know him, intimately and personally, beyond words and thoughts. And the best way to do that is *vacare Deo*, spending time with God every day, with no agenda except to take a vacation with God.

8. PRAYING THE PSALMS

M uch of the monks' prayer together in choir is composed of the singing and reciting of the ancient biblical psalms. The psalms have always been the mainstay of the Liturgy of the Hours prayed by monks and other religious, and by priests and deacons. Today laypeople are using this prayer of the Church more and more as well. The psalms have also become more familiar to Catholics in general because of the expansion of their use in the Mass after the Second Vatican Council.

Praying the psalms reminds us of our heritage in the spiritual journey of our Israelite ancestors in the faith and above all connects us to the prayer practice of Jesus and the apostles, who prayed these same inspired texts throughout their lives.

The psalms have continued to be cherished by Jews and Christians for 2,500 years, which is proof of their constant effectiveness in the life of prayer and the search for God. They can speak to the vital realities in life, in personal suffering and anxiety, and in thirst for the divine, because these are constants in human life over the centuries. But because they are from an ancient world and culture, the psalms present special challenges for modern users.

The most important thing to realize about the psalms is that they are poetry. In some of the first English translations, the poetic nature of the psalms was obscured because they were printed in prose form. But today we can see the poetic form at a glance.

However, the psalms do not appear in the familiar form of rhymed couplets, and many of the characteristic qualities of poetry in the sounds and groupings of words, though present in the original Hebrew, can rarely be produced in translation. There are two qualities of Hebrew poetry, though, which appear in any language and can be used profitably to enliven the praying of the psalms: the parallelism and the imagery.

In the early centuries, the psalms were typically recited by heart. Manuscripts were expensive and few. The memorization was facilitated by the rhythm of the psalms, based on a line of two or three beats, and often arranged in a two-line sequence in which the second line repeats the content of the first, though using other words:

> The LORD is close to the brokenhearted,
>> saves those whose spirit is crushed. (Psalm 34:19)

> My feet were on the point of stumbling;
>> a little further and I should have slipped. (Psalm 73:2, Jerusalem Bible)

Sometimes the second line contrasts the first:

> Even if my father and mother forsake me,
>> the LORD will take me in. (Psalm 27:10)

This movement creates the effect of one wave following another.

Another poetic element that moves the psalm along and also carries and enriches the theme is the succession of images. The thought of a psalm is rarely expressed solely in ideas or conceptually, as we are accustomed to, but is embodied in images. We can say God protects, feeds, guides, doctors, carries, loves, and shelters me, or we can say, like the psalmist, "The LORD is my shepherd" (Psalm 23:1). On a bad day, we may feel like a sagging fence (62:4) or a broken dish (31:13). We yearn for God like parched land (63:2) or a thirsty deer (42:2). When things press in, we pray, "In the shadow of your wings I take refuge / until the destroying storms pass by" (57:1, NRSV).

Someone has remarked that monastic choirs are among the last places on earth where poetry is still recited on a daily basis. Even though they are poems, psalms may be prayed as prose, but the most natural way is to pray them as what they are. This means that we let ourselves be carried by the rhythmic beat and repetition of the verses, and by the images that appear and capture our imagination, and then move on. The effect is of a healing stream washing over us.

The psalms are ideal for the structure of the Liturgy of the Hours, which is different from that of the sacramental rites fashioned to build to a climax through a series of steps. The Mass, for example, has a definite structure in which various parts follow one another in a progression. There are several climactic points: the Gospel, the Presentation of Gifts, the Consecration, the Great Amen, Communion. Each part is important in building the whole and cannot be omitted, and the ritual demands a certain attention to the progression. An Hour of the Office has parts, but there is no climax as such. Our attention may be now

to the words, now to the rhythm, now to the images, but attention to the progression of the rite is less critical. Rather, we stand
together in the presence of God, opening ourselves to the saving
grace that rolls over us and carries us along.

9 . PRAY AND WORK

Benedictine monasticism is known far and wide for the motto "Pray and Work," in Latin, *Ora et Labora*. This motto bespeaks a balanced approach, and visitors to Benedictine monasteries are impressed by the rhythms that flow through the life of the monks. At times the work of the monks may make even more of an impression than the prayer, since the latter would be taken for granted in a search for God, and there is still a fair amount of attitude afloat that equates "spiritual" with "ethereal" or "angelic." St. Benedict's appreciation of the physical and the body in the spiritual program is refreshing.

It might come as a surprise to find out that *Ora et Labora* is not in the *Rule of St. Benedict*, and has only been in circulation as a Benedictine motto since the nineteenth century. Its staying power since that time shows that the phrase captures something attractive about the Benedictine life. There is a time for prayer and there is a time for work, and they are not the same thing. Benedict would never say, "My work is my prayer," though he would insist that our work should be inspired by the grace of our prayer, and that we can pray while we work.

The motto *Ora et Labora*, if interpreted as a division between the hours of public prayer (Divine Office) and the hours of work, leaves out an important third element in the monastic life described in the *Rule*. Anywhere from two to four hours in the daily schedule are allotted to the personal spiritual search using the practice called *lectio* (reading) or *lectio divina* (divine or holy reading). The *Ora* of the motto might be expanded to include *lectio*, since this practice is more prayer than simple reading or study. But the third vital element is usually just overlooked in the popular imagination. There is a church painting of St. Benedict that shows him holding an open book, on one page the word *Opus* (for *Opus Dei*, the Work of God, Benedict's favorite term for the Divine Office), and on the other *Labora*, daily work, as if these two exercises encompassed the life of the monk.

The danger in dividing the monk's (or anybody's) day into public prayer and assigned work is that it leaves out the whole area of private prayer, the monk's personal daily communion with God, which is what the balanced schedule is supposed to foster in the first place.

But whatever the popular perception of this Benedictine motto, people who are attracted to Benedictine spirituality or visit monasteries are not fooled. They pick up instinctively the priority of the personal in the monks' search for God and are drawn to spend private time in prayer and *lectio* themselves. A balanced life needs all three elements: a time for prayer in community, a time for private prayer, and a time for work. Unless you live in a monastery or are close enough to a church for daily Mass, prayer in community is often infrequent, perhaps weekly. But this can be enough for most people. The important thing is to be sure that there is daily personal communion with God, being "alone with the alone." This builds the interior foundation that enriches public prayer, even if infrequent, but without the daily search for God, prayer in community finds its heart fading.

The monastic rhythm assures that the whole person—physical, mental, spiritual—is involved in the daily search for God, and that the elements interpenetrate. There are not hermetically sealed compartments separating prayer from work and the other necessary activities of the life. Benedict reminds us that "the divine presence is everywhere," and emphasizes that this is "especially true when we celebrate the divine office" (*Rule of Benedict,* 19:1-2). But he also wants the utensils and goods of the monastery to be treated as "sacred vessels of the altar" (31:10). If our public or private prayer happens to be interrupted by a visitor at the door, our communion with God is not therefore interrupted, because the guest is welcomed as Christ (53:1). The spirit is the same as that captured by the Carmelite Brother Lawrence of the Resurrection, who found God in the pots and pans of his kitchen.

10. *LECTIO DIVINA*: WHAT IS IT?

In the Christian prayer tradition, there are two important spiritual disciplines focused on reading: spiritual reading and *lectio divina* (divine or holy reading). Spiritual reading has been well known in recent centuries, but *lectio divina*, an ancient practice associated with Benedictine monasticism, has only recently entered the common spiritual vocabulary. We are already familiar with spiritual reading, and because "holy reading" sounds similar, we may think it is the same. But the practices are distinct and have different purposes.

What we know as spiritual reading was practically impossible before the invention of the printing press in 1440. Spiritual reading depends on the availability of many books, but before 1440, books were extremely rare and very expensive, requiring a large supply of animal skins and months of labor by skilled copyists. It is estimated that a single Bible produced that way would cost at least twenty thousand dollars today.

On the other hand, the practice known as *lectio divina* belongs in its origins to the preprinting era, and though not impossible today, it is difficult for us because it requires learning to read the way people did when texts were rare and scarce. Because we live in a world of accessible texts, whether in printed or electronic form, we have been trained to read quickly and even aggressively, milking a text of its information and moving on. We have less and less need or appetite for storing texts in our memory because they are only a fingertip away. We don't have time to turn words and phrases over and over in our minds because another shipment is already at the door.

Spiritual reading and *lectio divina* have different purposes, but they are complementary. In general, spiritual reading is focused on information and serves as a background for *lectio divina*, which seeks transformation and union with God beyond words. Spiritual reading refers to any reading we do for information or inspiration about God, the Church, or the spiritual life. It is an intellectual pursuit, providing the background for the search for God as well as the stimulus and encouragement to pursue it: Church history, the lives of the saints, the ways of prayer.

Lectio divina is more about experiencing God than thinking about him, and about being washed by the word of God rather than reflecting on it. Its literature is not new writings to generate thinking, but the old and familiar that favor mulling, which is why the Bible (a "sacred reading" in itself) is the favored text. In contemporary usage, *lectio* often integrates old and new methods of "reading" in a practice of "holy loafing" with the Bible, using the textual apparatus and technical assistance now available. *Lectio divina* is not complete until it ends in prayer, and at its highest level is contemplative silence in the presence of God.

It has become customary to think of *lectio divina* in terms of the four steps described by Prior Guigo II in the twelfth century: *lectio, meditatio, oratio*, and *contemplatio*— reading, meditation, prayer, and contemplation. This is a logical progression, but these steps are not necessarily followed in each session of *lectio divina*, nor in this order. A person may go directly to contemplation (or any of the steps), and stay there or go forward or backward.

The first two steps are preparation for prayer. The last two are prayer—in the first case, prayer with words; in the second, prayer of silent presence. The kind of reading this exercise envisions is illuminated by an understanding of "meditation," which in this practice does not mean the reflective exercise with which modern people are familiar. *Meditatio* here has its ancient meaning of the repetition of a holy word over and over in the mind and even on the tongue to savor it. Another word applied to this practice was *ruminatio*, chewing the cud. One medieval monk reported to another that his *lectio* was hampered by a sore throat.

A practice of *lectio* utilizing the four steps in their traditional order might look like this: reading—Romans 12:9, "Let love be sincere"; then meditation—repeating the verse again and again as if washing oneself with the word; then prayer—a petition like "Jesus, help me to love sincerely"; and finally, contemplation—resting in the Lord beyond words. But it is usually not this formal. *Lectio divina* is very free and adaptable to each person's style and to the situation of the day. It is a way of sitting comfortably with the word of God, opening ourselves to God, heart to heart, and waiting for communion. The word does not even have to be "read" in the modern sense: after years of familiarity with Scripture in personal devotion and the sacramental life of the Church, the word of God is already within us and ready for interior reading. ∽

11. *LECTIO DIVINA:* WHAT IS IT FOR?

J esus' journey to Jerusalem in the synoptic gospels is a model for the spiritual journey of Christian disciples. At different times we may see ourselves on the road with Jesus or as one of the people who meet him along the way. The healing of the blind beggar by the side of the road (Mark 10:46-52; Luke 18:35-43) throws light on themes of the monastic life, which St. Benedict presents as a journey and as a pursuit of true sight: "Let us set out on this way, with the Gospel for our guide, that we may be worthy to see him who has called us to his kingdom" (*Rule of Benedict*, Prologue, 21). A few verses earlier, he had admonished: "Let us open our eyes to the light that comes from God" (Prologue, 9).

The blind man wants to see but is rebuked by "the people walking in front" (Luke 18:39). A world blinded by sin conspires to keep us all from seeing. The media culture keeps us busy, keeps our minds distracted, so that we will not concentrate on the things that really matter. Twice the blind man cries out: "*Kyrie, eleison!*"—"Jesus, Son of David, have pity on me." The third time he cries: "Lord, please let me see!" Jesus says, "Have sight; your faith has saved you" (Luke 18:38-42).

We need to see clearly to make our way to Jerusalem with Jesus. There are so many things in our lives that don't make sense, but often we are confused because we don't know how to look at them, really to see and understand them. The monastic practice of *lectio divina* is designed to help us gain our sight, or to recover it. The cry of the blind beggar may also be translated as "Lord, that I may see again!"—that is, recover the sight that I had lost along the way.

In *lectio divina* we open ourselves to the word of God so that we may "put on the Lord Jesus Christ" (Romans 13:14) and have "the mind of Christ" (1 Corinthians 2:16). This is not an intellectual exercise like Scripture study; rather, the slow and repetitive reading of this practice is like a mother hen sitting on eggs waiting for them to hatch. You cannot hurry the result—no speed-reading. Catholic historian Eamon Duffy described it as "loitering with intent."

Jesus said at one point, "Blessed are your eyes, because they see" (Matthew 13:16). This is not the same as saying we are blessed because of what we see, though that is also true: "Blessed are the eyes that see what you see" (Luke 10:23). But the seeing of the first saying is the gift to see with "the light that comes from God" (*Rule of Benedict*, Prologue, 9), to see the world and people the way God sees them. *Lectio divina* leads to "divine reading," being able to read reality the way God does. The saints are those who learned to see this way. "Lord, that I may see!"

True seeing in this way is not a matter of intellectual clarity. More study will not bring it about. *Lectio divina* aims at the roots of our spiritual eyes, which are in our heart. It pours the word over us and drenches us through and through. The process is well captured in a story from the desert fathers.

A young man had tried to turn his life around but was at his wit's end. He approached a desert monk renowned for care of souls. The monk listened to his story and gave him a cave where he could pray and read Scripture. The young man tried it for awhile but noticed no progress. He forgot what he read; he felt too listless to pray; he fell asleep in the midst of his reading. The monk gave him a wicker basket and told him to fill it with sand, place it outside the door, and every day pour a bucket of water over the sand. The young man did so, and found that every time he poured water over the sand, some of the sand leaked out of the basket. After weeks and months of prayer and reading and pouring water over the sand, one day he found the basket clean. He reported this to his spiritual father and the monk said, "My son, you are the basket. The sand is your sinfulness, your pride, your unhappiness. The water is the word of God. The basket doesn't remember the water that gradually cleansed it. Neither do you remember every word of holy Scripture that you read. But if you continue to pour the water of God's word over your sinfulness, someday you, too, will be clean."

12. Overshadowed by a Cloud

Over the years I have given many talks on prayer. Invariably what attracts the most attention is the subject of distractions in prayer and how to deal with them. I try to stress that distractions are not that important, that they are very overrated. They don't mean your prayer is bad.

This isn't an original idea; it goes way back in the tradition. I agree with Thomas Merton's comment: "If you've never had distractions, you don't know how to pray." We don't notice the stream of thoughts and imagination constantly going on in our mind until we try to shut it down to focus on God.

But unless we have a rare gift of mind control, we can't put distractions out of our minds. The human mind is naturally very active and creative, and modern methods of education are designed to make our minds even more aggressive and inquisitive. Could we really expect to be able to shut down this mental activity just because we want to pray?

One of my favorite images about distractions is the one about the monkeys in the tree. Whenever you sit or kneel down to pray, you inevitably find yourself under a tree full of monkeys. The monkeys are your thoughts, and they keep swinging and chattering, trying to get you to join them in the tree. If you suddenly notice yourself swinging with them, simply slide back down under the tree and let the monkeys play above you. The wrong solution is to try to silence the monkeys and make them quit swinging—which is impossible anyway—because then they will have our full attention.

The purity of prayer is measured not by the clarity of the focus but by the intensity of the desire. If I come into the presence of God for the purpose of praying and don't change my intention, the time I spend is all prayer, no matter what distractions I encounter. It's hard for us to believe this truth because we feel guilty at the end of a distracted prayer time and think it was time wasted. At least if we attended Mass, or prayed an hour of the Divine Office, or spoke words to God, or recited prayers we know by heart, we could point to what we have done. But at the end of a time spent trying to focus on God in silence, we do not know what we have done.

But just because we cannot tell what we have done during the time of prayer does not mean we have done nothing, and it certainly doesn't mean God has done nothing. God is intimately present during prayer but does not always warm us with the feeling of his nearness. That would defeat the purpose. If our prayer is to bring us to the interior freedom of true discipleship, we must give up control and rely completely on God. Our ignorance of what we are doing in prayer and our struggle with distractions are part of God's strategy: they help to humble us and throw us back on the mercy of God. "He must increase; I must decrease" (John 3:30).

A few of the saints of Christian history have had gifts of ecstasy in prayer, in which they felt at times taken out of themselves and completely absorbed in God. These types of experiences have attracted a lot of attention and led to the mistaken idea that they are typical of "real prayer" or of the prayer of all the saints. Such stories stand out because they are rare. Even the saints who received these special gifts experienced this kind of prayer only rarely, and spent most of their prayer time with the same struggles as the rest of us. There is also a strong tradition of darkness in prayer among the saints—St. Thérèse of Lisieux, for example, and more recently, Padre Pio and Mother Teresa.

In earlier chapters I have often quoted an anonymous English monk in the fourteenth-century book very appropriately entitled *The Cloud of Unknowing*. Between us and God is a cloud that we cannot penetrate by knowledge but that we can penetrate by love, or what the author calls the "darts of love" in prayer. We are plagued by distractions, but without anxiety, we can simply relegate them to the "cloud of forgetting." "Learn to be at home in this darkness, . . . letting your spirit cry out to him whom you love" (3).

Distractions in prayer turn out after all not to be a curse but a blessing. They keep us from seeking the wrong goal in prayer, and they make us humble. The struggle they cause tests and strengthens our desire for God. Ultimately, distractions, instead of blocking or limiting our prayer, purify our love for God and help us keep our attention focused on him.

Part III

Calling and Commitment

13. THE DEFAULT SETTING

The computer age has spawned a lot of new vocabulary—blog, Web site, toolbar—and provided new applications for terms we already knew. One of the latter is "default," not in its sense of failure, but in the usage "by default," when a substitution is made automatically for something else when circumstances change. (Webster gives the example "remained the club's president by default.")

In computer language, "default setting" means an option that will be chosen automatically by the machine when a choice has not been specified by the operator: for example, the word processor's type font, margins, and indentations. The default setting may be overridden at any time, and then the new option will remain in force throughout the current operation. But when a new document or project is begun, the machine will return automatically to the default setting. This is a great aid in freeing the operator from having to respecify the preferred program settings when changing projects.

Any major decision and commitment about our own life should proceed in the same way. When we decide to be a Christian, to marry, to profess monastic vows, or to be ordained, our lives should adopt the "default setting" that goes with the commitment. A married person's default setting prevents romantic involvement with a third person; a monk's default setting rules out large spending and acquisition without permission. Certain options or opportunities arise, and we know immediately if they are compatible with our default setting. The commitment is interior, but it has consequences in the way we live. And the way we live is a series of choices about our actions.

For one thing, the default settings in our lives save us a lot of time, just as they do with the computer. When new opportunities or offers arise, most of the time we know immediately whether or not they are compatible with our life commitments. When the issue is not that clear, we can look at the opportunity more closely for discernment. But we don't waste a lot of time and energy going down dead ends, or worse, pursuing options that would contradict a commitment carefully made and, as a result, cause a shipwreck in our lives. A frequent theme in literature is the self-inflicted tragedy caused by departure from one's ethics and best instincts, as in *Macbeth*, one of the many reflections on the more far-reaching story of Adam and Eve.

The recommendation of a default setting in a life based on chosen principles might seem obvious to those of us who live within a firm tradition of faith and life, but it is not obvious at all in the world at large. In fact, to many it seems crazy—confining, deadly, smothering the excitement of living. What about adventure, experimentation, keeping one's options open? What about personal freedom?

The choosing of default settings in life is the highest exercise of personal freedom. It is the difference between deciding from within myself how I will live and being pushed and pulled by external forces: trends, tragedies, or relationships. Our effort should be to grow into free human beings who are not tossed about by the next event in our lives, but who evaluate and respond to the surprises—good and bad—from a stable center. The freedom comes in evaluating the traditions and norms handed down from preceding generations and determining which ones will guide our lives. Lack of personal freedom is exposed in the inability to live by the chosen norm, the default setting. To be cut loose and drifting gives the illusion of freedom, but it provides no more ability to negotiate the challenges of life than a boat without a rudder trying to find its way among the rocks in the stream.

It takes an intelligent operator to program a computer to its various default settings, but once they are set, the computer adheres mindlessly to the instructions it has been given. We use our intelligence, our faith, and our personal freedom to adopt a default setting that will enable us to live faithfully the vocation we have chosen and accepted. We do not adopt the setting mindlessly, however, and we can override it at any time. But since we have chosen it with care, we will rarely need to tinker with it, and it will act as an ongoing support in our freedom to serve the Lord. ∽⌒

14 . Living from Decision

St. Benedict makes it difficult for newcomers to enter the monastery. He is straightforward about this practice, beginning in chapter 58 on "The Procedure for Receiving Brothers," with this admonition: "Do not grant newcomers to the monastic life an easy entry, but, as the Apostle says, 'Test the spirits to see if they are from God'" (l John 4:1). Then he keeps the newcomers knocking for four or five days to test their patience and perseverance. This seems quite at odds with his open-arms approach to the stranger in chapter 53 on receiving guests.

But for both the random guest and the monastic seeker, Benedict has their best interests at heart. Occasional guests need to be assured of acceptance because of their inherent worth as children of God (as Christ), but applicants to the monastery, who are also received as Christ, must be reminded immediately of the seriousness of what they are asking. Benedict is not making entry hard for them because of some prejudice about their social status or race. Each applicant receives the same treatment as any other. Later, as monks, they will continue to be treated fairly, ranked in the community not on the basis of their age, family, education, or social rank but simply by their date of entrance.

Benedict wants the newcomers to know that they are asking for something that will change their whole lives. If they decide to stay and commit themselves as Benedictine monks, from that day every decision they make will be affected by their monastic profession. The profession formula is presented in St. Benedict's

Rule as a promise of stability, *conversatio morum*, and obedience. Stability binds the monk to a particular community in a particular place; obedience puts him under the authority of the superior; and *conversatio morum*, translated today as "fidelity to the monastic way of life" (or "monastic lifestyle"), commits the monk to living thoroughly the "common life" of the particular community. This latter element involves celibate chastity and community of goods, specified in other orders as chastity and poverty, and also all the rituals and exercises that compose the life: the Work of God (official community prayer), personal prayer and *lectio divina,* silence, mutual obedience, community meals and meeting, and monastic clothing.

There is a true sense that the monk professes to be obedient to the schedule of the monastery as the voice of God calling him throughout the day. This is not for the purpose of making robots but gradually to bring inner liberation from the ego of control. The monk must learn to let go of his own agenda time after time, day after day, for love of God.

Idealistically, there is only one vocation decision necessary in the monastic life, the one made on the day of profession when the monk promised stability, fidelity to the monastic way of life, and obedience once and for all for the rest of his life. Everything that follows flows from that decision: where I am to be and what I am to be doing. All the decisions that are part of my assignment also partake of that vocation commitment. Obviously, this attitude is more of a goal than a starting point, and it is the work of a lifetime. When I stand with my brothers in choir, ideally it is not a new decision at this hour but the application of a decision made years ago and now being acted upon.

There is an obvious comparison with the state of marriage. Everything changed for the couple on the day of their wedding. Now they are two in one flesh and cannot make significant decisions independently of one another and their children. Every decision they make should flow from the big decision made at their wedding. Marriage partners who realize this truth early on in their marriage, and monks who realize it about their own vocation decision, are very unlikely to begin drifting away from their commitment. Their decision holds them, not the feelings that come and go.

Sometimes we should mentally review our profession charts or the formulas pronounced at marriage to see whether any asterisks have been added since we made our commitment. We might find that our commitment is not as strong as it was at the beginning, because along the way we have added asterisks making exceptions: I will do this "except" in certain cases; or "yes, but not all the time." These small exceptions gradually erode the commitment and steal away the peace and happiness of living our lives as a daily gift flowing from a freely made decision. ৩৫

15. SEEKING GOD

In chapter 58 of his *Rule* on "The Procedure for Receiving Brothers," St. Benedict instructs the novice director to devote careful attention to the newcomer who is trying to learn the ways of the monastic life, and first of all to see whether the candidate is truly seeking God.

That may seem a strange thing to mention. It should go without saying that someone seeking entrance to a monastery would be seeking God. But of course it is not automatically so. The novice may have a mistaken idea of God, of himself, and of the purpose of the monastic life, and it may take some time and considerable assistance to sort it all out.

To be truly seeking God, however, is not in itself a sign of a monastic vocation. People who are even somewhat religious would describe themselves as seeking God. But how do any of us know that it is really God we are seeking? Perhaps under the guise of searching for God, we might be subtly seeking something else instead of or in addition to God: security, for example, or prestige or position. And how do we stay focused on the true search once we have embarked upon it?

St. Benedict goes on to instruct the novice director to be on the lookout to see whether the newcomer is solicitous—even eager—for three things: the Work of God, obedience, and trials. These norms have a monastic flavor, but they are adaptable in various ways to all who are seeking God. All three test whether we are willing, not just once but on a daily basis, to take our hands off the handlebars and let God be in charge.

Work of God (*Opus Dei*) is Benedict's preferred term for the Divine Office, the hours of common prayer for which the monks gather several times a day. This becomes a major touchstone for the validity of the monk's observance: "Nothing is to be preferred to the Work of God" (*Rule of Benedict*, 43:3). It is easy enough for anyone to say God comes before everything else in my life, but I may be fooling myself. It may be all in my head. Do I come to the end of the day and find I have not made room for God? In the case of a monk, when the bell rings, am I able to interrupt what I am doing to join the community in prayer? The true test comes during prime time, the middle of the workday. Is my work more important to me than God's work? I may find I am more committed to the noon meal than to the noon prayer. My mind and my tongue may deceive me, but my feet tell me the truth.

Obedience goes very much against the grain of self-will. Why should I take instructions from someone who is no better or smarter than I? No good reason other than the best: that the one in authority takes the place of Christ for me—not because of his merits but because of God's appointment through the election of the community and because of my free choice to accept this authority in faith. This holds true for everyone in the larger Church, where the same pattern is at work: God's will being communicated through human agents, who are by definition weak. It is a great school of humility and opens us to interior freedom.

"Trials" is a translation of the Latin *opprobria*, which is variously also rendered as hardships or humiliations. Is the novice ready to accept whatever comes and to trust God's daily providence without murmuring (a favorite word in the *Rule*)? Or does he have to constantly seek self-justification or retribution for slights? Benedict does not see trials as an interruption of God's work in our lives, but as an important part of the process. They are the cross breaking in. For Benedict, seeking God is not tested on the grand scale but moment to moment. Am I able to break away from my own pursuits, my own ideas, my own hurts—right now—to turn myself over to the Lord?

16. MUTUAL OBEDIENCE

People generally associate religious life in the Church with the profession of poverty, chastity, and obedience, and that is accurate, because those three virtues are fundamental to religious profession in all orders. But it is not that simple for the Benedictine monastic profession. In the *Rule of Benedict*, the triad of the profession formula is stability, *conversatio,* and obedience. Poverty and chastity fall under *conversatio,* which has no one-word equivalent in English but means "the monastic way of life."

Religious obedience is typically understood as the willingness to accept direction and assignments from a religious superior who acts with God's authority for the vowed member. It is, therefore, a vertical relationship between the one giving orders and the one obeying them.

This is certainly true for the Benedictine life. The abbot is believed to represent Christ in the monastery, and all other superiors in the monastery embody this Christ-role when they share his authority. Vertical obedience to God through the superior is part of the bedrock of the *Rule of Benedict.*

But there is another important dimension to Benedictine obedience, described this way in chapter 71 of the *Rule:* "Obedience is a blessing to be shown by all, not only to the abbot but also to one another as brothers, since we know that it is by this way of obedience that we go to God" (71:1-2). Benedictine obedience is not fulfilled by simply obeying the commands of the abbot or someone acting on his authority. That is fundamental, but it is not sufficient.

The meaning of this "mutual obedience" is illuminated in chapter 72, where part of "The Good Zeal of Monks" is "earnestly competing in obedience to one another" (72:6), an expression that is framed by a quote from St. Paul with an application: "'They should each try to be the first to show respect to the other' (Romans 12:10), supporting with the greatest patience one another's weaknesses of body or behavior. . . . No one is to pursue what he judges better for himself but instead, what he judges better for someone else" (72:4-7).

In legislating for monastic obedience, Benedict is invoking an aspect of gospel obedience that is of fundamental importance for the spiritual journey, and not only in monasteries.

What St. Benedict has done is to show that gospel obedience, however it is observed, has to be animated by both of the great commandments: love of God and love of neighbor. The understanding of love of neighbor as part of obedience is a creative insight. It emphasizes that God's will enters our lives not only in commands from above but also in interactions with one another. In his *Shorter Rules* (115), St. Basil, an earlier monastic teacher, uses the words of Jesus and Paul to interpret mutual obedience: "The Son of Man came not to be served but to serve" (Mark 10:45, NRSV); "Through love of the Spirit be servants to one another" (see Galatians 5:13).

Sometimes this means that we will do what we are asked by another brother or sister, but more often the "commands" of mutual obedience are unspoken, the response of love in sensitivity to the needs of another, "supporting with the greatest patience one another's weaknesses of body and behavior." In the practice of mutual obedience, God shows his will day by day, minute by minute, through the needs of our brothers and sisters, who represent Christ in our daily life. You will not be completely obedient to God by doing what you are told by authority and nothing more.

The members of a monastic community are not together by accident. Each has responded to a call from God to join this group in a common search for God. For a Benedictine, mutual obedience is a central part of the living of stability: this particular group of people mediates God's will to me. Providence has called us together from all eternity and for all eternity.

But this is not unique to monastic communities. The same call to mutual obedience is part of the family unit, created by God when he called the man and woman together in marriage and then gave them children. Each one of them represents Christ to the other, and they are constantly relying on one another for help and support in their daily lives. These are not only random needs and random requests. As in the monastery, these are opportunities to draw closer to God day by day and minute by minute in the exercise of mutual obedience. ∽⌒

17. THE NOONDAY DEVIL

wonderful passage in the *Institutes* of John Cassian (360–435), a monastic source for St. Benedict, catches a monk in the middle of the day, experiencing the tedium of his life:

> He dreams of monasteries a long way off, and describes such places as more profitable and better suited for salvation; and he paints the life of the community there as beautiful and full of spiritual life. On the other hand, he says that everything around him is rough, and there is nothing edifying in the brothers who live with him. He imagines that he will never be well unless he leaves as quickly as possible. He sighs that none of the community ever come to visit him, and he often goes in and out of his cell, gazing at the sun as if it was too slow in setting. (Book X, chapter 2)

The Latin term for this malady is *acedia*, which Cassian defines as "weariness or distress of heart." It is akin to the capital sin of sloth. A scriptural reference was seen in Psalm 91:6, which mentions "the sickness that lays waste at midday," but its flavor was best captured by the monk and desert father Evagrius (346–399) as the "noonday devil."

Noonday refers to the middle of the day, but it may also mean the middle of life, with the noonday devil as a vivid image for the midlife crisis. There is a weariness that may settle in with the monotony of life day after day. Is this all there is? St. Paul knew the feeling and encouraged the Galatians: "Let us not grow weary of doing good" (6:9, NAB 1970). Poet Robert Frost speaks of the dawn—of the day, of life, of any new beginning—as gold which slips away in the heat of noon: "So dawn goes down to day. / Nothing gold can stay."

How do we deal with this noonday devil wherever it attacks us—in the heat and drudgery of a particular day, or in the middle of our monastic life or marriage, or in the monotony of the work that we do for a living? Is there a way to hold on to the vision, the hope, the joy that we had at dawn? Was the dawn a mirage and midday the reality?

The early monastic teachers would say that both dawn and midday are realities, and that there is mirage in both of them. There is a certain amount of illusion in the excitement of the new, but there is also a reflexive pessimism that makes it hard to see the blessing in the ordinary, in the same old thing.

The noonday devil wants to make us run away from our commitment to look for a greener pasture. The monastic teachers tell us that the way to defeat that devil is to sit still, to recommit, to stay with the task. Especially do they tell us to stay with the Lord: not just discipline, but spiritual discipline. St. Benedict makes "stability" one of the three ingredients of his profession formula, along with obedience and *conversatio morum* (the monastic way of living). His *Rule* establishes a pattern that supports the personal search for God in the regularity of exercises in the brotherhood, hour after hour and day after day. The search is not sporadic or selective; it goes on all the time in everything.

St. Benedict is constantly calling the monks back into focus by having them come together for community prayer seven times during the day and once at night: "We should praise our Creator for his just judgment at these times: Lauds, Prime, Terce, Sext, None, Vespers, and Compline; and let us arise at night to give him praise" (*Rule of Benedict*, 16:5). There is time for manual or other work, and time allotted for the private spiritual work of *lectio divina*. When followed day after day over a period of time, a rhythm is set that carries the monk forward. But it isn't only that. The schedule teaches the monk to put God first at every hour. This attitude defeats the noonday devil because it is an attitude of hope.

Every life needs a hopeful spiritual discipline that recognizes the presence and action of God at all times. It is often in the middle of the day, or in the middle of a task, that we lose sight of what is really going on. We don't like the interruption and brush it aside. But the interruption is often a person, a child breaking into a mother's work, or a brother in need when I am in a hurry in the hallway. This is where God breaks in, but where the noonday devil is also lurking.

St. Benedict emphasizes the presence of God everywhere and at every moment, but "beyond the least doubt we should believe this to be especially true when we celebrate the divine office" (*Rule of Benedict*, 19:2). Because of this, he makes it a cardinal rule that "nothing is to be preferred to the Work of God" (43:3). A monk learns that the test of his faith is not in the great hours of morning and evening prayer, but in the noonday prayer, the prayer that interrupts the day. It costs more to break away in the middle of a task. The noonday devil is sorting out the major and minor leaguers. And so it is with the life of everyone. The noonday devil can sleep at the beginning or end of the day, when pressure of interruption is rare or light. He saves his energy for the time of the heat, when our defenses are down. ᏡᏡ

Part IV

The Christian Life

18. BAPTIZED INTO HIS DEATH

A standard choice as a Mass reading at Catholic funerals is from chapter 6 of St. Paul's Letter to the Romans, which contains this sentence: "Are you unaware that we who were baptized into Christ Jesus were baptized into his death?" (6:3). In the context of the funeral, the implication could be that the bereaved can be consoled to know that the departed loved one, because of baptism, has shared in a special way in the physical death of Jesus.

But that is not what it means. A few verses further on, Paul says, "If we have grown into union with him through a death like his, we shall also be united with him in the resurrection" (Romans 6:5). All of us die, but there is something unique about the death of Jesus. All will die, but not all will have *a death like his*. Paul speaks similarly in his Letter to the Philippians of his goal "to know him and the power of his resurrection and the sharing of his sufferings by being *conformed to his death*" (3:10). There is something special about the death of Jesus.

St. Thomas Aquinas tells us what this is in his commentary on Romans 5:10: "We were reconciled to God by the death of his Son because of its special qualities . . . : that Christ willed to die out of obedience to the Father and out of love for our brothers and sisters." This interior gift of love and obedience, which animated Jesus' entire life, culminated in his complete self-gift on Calvary. It is this death into which we were baptized.

When referring to the death of Jesus in us, Paul often prefers the language of "dying" to emphasize that it is a growing daily reality. We are "always carrying about in the body the dying of Jesus, so that the life of Jesus may also be manifested in our body" (2 Corinthians 4:10). As our lives are more and more governed by self-giving love and obedience, we become conformed to the death of Jesus. Then the interior dying begins to affect our visible living, letting the rays of resurrection shine through. All the slights and misunderstandings, the aches and pains, the delays and postponements of the day, instead of being fodder for complaining, can be transformed into the dying and rising victory of Christ in us. "For we who live are constantly being given up to death for the sake of Jesus, so that the life of Jesus may be manifested in our mortal flesh" (4:11).

We are baptized *into* the death of Christ. There is a movement, like the plunge into the baptismal waters, but the movement is only beginning at baptism. We embark on a life of dying with Jesus, opening ourselves to the divine power of grace to empty us steadily of the selfish disobedience we inherited from Adam and to fill us with the loving obedience of Jesus. Of course, this "dying" is really living life to the fullest, with the gifts of the Spirit, and in utter human freedom. Our hope is that by the time we reach the end of our earthly lives, the death of our physical bodies will be an external sign of what has been going on inside. In the saints, this has been true in a dramatic way, but only in Jesus has it been perfect. His physical death was like a sacramental sign of what was really happening inside him.

In the divine plan for all of us, the only way to resurrection and life with God is through dying with Jesus. It is not simply a matter of death now and resurrection later. Death and resurrection both begin now in our earthly life, and they are intertwined.

Resurrection will shine in our lives if we are giving ourselves with loving obedience to Jesus, but otherwise, even though our life may look shiny on the surface, there is no dying inside, and we are only "a resounding gong or a clashing cymbal" (1 Corinthians 13:1).

When St. Paul speaks of being baptized into the death of Jesus, he is using different words to say what Jesus himself said: "Whoever wishes to come after me must deny himself, take up his cross, and follow me" (Mark 8:34). The dying of Jesus and the cross are the way to joy and to eternal life. In a beautiful meditation, St. Francis de Sales tells us what a gift it is to have been baptized into the death of Christ:

The everlasting God has in his wisdom foreseen from all eternity the cross that he now presents to you as a gift from his inmost heart. This cross he now sends you he has considered with his all-knowing eyes, understood with his divine mind, tested with his wise justice, warmed with loving arms, and weighed with his own hands, to see that it be not one inch too large and not one ounce too heavy for you. He has blessed it with his holy name, anointed it with his grace, perfumed it with his consolation, taken one last glance at you and your courage, and then sent it to you from heaven, a special greeting from God to you, an alms of the all-merciful love of God.

19. YIELD

D r. Susan Muto, a specialist in spiritual formation, was once asked to write a series of short articles on what she considered the top ten spiritual classics in Western spirituality. On her list were writers who would be on anyone's top ten—St. Augustine, St. John of the Cross, St. Teresa of Ávila—but at the top was a surprise. The number one classic for Dr. Muto was *Abandonment to Divine Providence* by Jean Pierre de Caussade, SJ.

This name and book may not be familiar to many contemporary readers. Fr. Caussade was the spiritual director of a community of Visitation Nuns in France in the eighteenth century. His conferences to this community were edited in 1861, a century after his death, under the title *Abandonment to Divine Providence* and have grown more and more influential ever since. Caussade's theme, presented in many different ways and from various angles, is that God is ever present with each one of us, showing his will to us in the circumstances of our daily lives, and that the way to holiness is to trust God and to yield to his active presence moment by moment. "Abandonment" in English has a more passive meaning than the French word it translates and can sound apathetic. But Caussade requires an active cooperation with grace in the everyday challenges, a more positive "yielding to God." His meaning is better captured in the new title adopted in recent years, *The Sacrament of the Present Moment*.

Caussade's teaching was part of a crescendo leading up to the declaration of the universal call to holiness at the Second Vatican Council (*Dogmatic Constitution on the Church*, chapter 5). Since the Middle Ages, there was an impression in the Church that there were different levels of expectation and possibility in the pursuit of holiness: that only those called to a special vocation in the Church should aspire to the highest levels of holiness. The first strong voice to challenge this theory was St. Francis de Sales in his *Introduction to the Devout Life* in the early seventeenth century. Later in the same century, another note was struck independently by Carmelite Brother Lawrence of the Resurrection in *The Practice of the Presence of God*. A few years later came Caussade, and then in the late nineteenth century, St. Thérèse of Lisieux, with her autobiography, *The Story of a Soul*. Both Caussade and St. Thérèse give credit to the influence of St. Francis.

All of these writers not only taught that holiness is available to all but showed a way that all could follow, whatever one's state in life. We are most familiar with it in St. Thérèse's "little way." God draws us to himself through the everyday things that come our way. All we have to do is try to bring the love of God to each moment of the day as it unfolds in each person and each task. It is very simple, but deceptively so, because it is also very demanding in its constant dedication to responding to every situation with love and integrity. It is a moment to moment yielding to the will of God manifested in the people and situations sent into our lives. Though it is presented as a path for those who can't walk the high road, it is really the road every saint must take. In Caussade's terms, it is receiving the sacrament of the present moment.

The secret to holiness is letting God reverse the pattern of Adam in us, letting pride and disobedience be replaced by humility and obedience, giving up control over our lives. We cannot do it ourselves, though we would like to control even the process of giving up control. To the fallen angel, Lucifer, is attributed the battle cry "I will not serve." And when a contest was held in hell to name the most popular song of the twentieth century, so the tale goes, the winning title was "I Did It My Way." But salvation is completely the work of God: it is all the work of grace, a gift we do not receive all at once but drop by drop and moment by moment. What we can control is our decision not to control, to yield to God, to surrender our lives.

In her classic meditation on Mary, *The Reed of God*, Caryll Houselander noted that Jesus' words in the garden, "Not my will but thine be done," bring to a culmination the response of Mary to the angel, "Be it done unto me according to thy word." Our salvation from beginning to end is a story of yielding to the will of God. ❧

20. Freedom

The story is told of the little boy who liked to watch his sister's goldfish swim around in its home, a bowl of water. But the more he thought about it, the more he didn't like that the fish was confined to such a small space and had no real freedom. So he got a hammer and broke the bowl to give the fish its freedom.

There is a lot of confusion about the meaning of freedom. On the Fourth of July, we speak about freedom and independence as if they were the same. It is helpful to distinguish freedom as a condition of the person, and liberty as a condition of the environment. There are many independent people who are not free and many dependent people who are. Henry David Thoreau and Nelson Mandela were completely free when they were behind bars, though they did not have liberty of movement, but some of the people who put them there, though they were at liberty to come and go as they chose, were not free.

Freedom is the prize of human maturity. It is meant for all but not achieved by all. It permits us to live by norms that we have chosen and internalized.

For many, freedom means the ability to act without external restrictions. This is the counterfeit of freedom that inspires the bizarre ideas and activities associated with TV talk shows. This understanding of freedom is partially true, but by missing a large part of the truth, it becomes false. True freedom involves being unbound also from the internal restrictions imposed by the unseen masters that drive decisions and actions: passions, fears, prejudices, resentments, insecurities. These hidden masters make us a prey for the external masters: opinion, fashion, social pressures, esteem of peers, influence of celebrities.

It is impossible for a human being to live without a master. We did not create ourselves. "You are not your own" (1 Corinthians 6:19). The free person is one who has decided on and chosen God as master. Slavery is serving a master you haven't chosen. St. Paul teaches that Christ has freed us from slavery to sin. But he goes on to say, "Freed from sin, you have become slaves of righteousness" (Romans 6:18). In other words, you have to choose one master or the other, sin or righteousness, or rather, sin or God. True human freedom begins when we recognize God's lordship over our lives and take the first steps to making God our master. St. Augustine says, "Whoever is not bound by this chain is a slave." The usual path to freedom begins from a desire for no restriction at all (better known as license), to a desire to be answerable to no external norm (such as the laws and restrictions of church and society), to a desire for a chosen internal norm that will direct our lives.

The role of the Ten Commandments is helpful in illustrating the journey to true freedom. The Commandments are external norms of behavior, but they are meant to become far more than that. They are presented twice in the Bible (Exodus 20:1-17; Deuteronomy 5:6-21), and both times are introduced with the words: "I, the LORD, am your God, who brought you out of the land of Egypt, that place of slavery." Then follow the "Ten Words," which tell us how to stay out of a deeper slavery. The translation "Commandments" is unfortunate, because it puts a negative slant on these Ten Words of God to us. They are meant to show us ways to live in freedom. If internalized, they become part of our inner norm grounded in God, whom we have chosen as our master. Until they become part of us, we are enslaved in our own egoism, living in the world as in a dangerous place, where people are adversaries who must be taken advantage of and overcome.

The lack of freedom ultimately causes a deep insecurity, a void which must be filled. It spawns jealousy and fear, and is the source of wars and quarrels, infidelities, and larcenies. Because I am empty, I try to fill up the vacancy by control of others, by possessions, by power. The more I receive of this kind of compensation, the more I need, because my insecurity is not being recognized and addressed at its source.

Ultimately, only God can heal us from insecurity and slavery and give us the gift of freedom, and God wants to do this—even "desperately"—and is very near and available. In communion with the Creator who made us and loves us, we begin to know our own worth and the worth of others, and we are free to accept ourselves and everyone else as we are, knowing that we are accepted by our loving Father. We are on the road to personal freedom. ∽

21. ALWAYS A LIFE FOR OTHERS

In his encyclical on hope, *Spe Salvi*, Pope Benedict XVI discussed the harsh critique Christianity sometimes receives when it is viewed as an individualistic search for salvation, a pursuit of one's own eternal happiness without regard to the plight of others. He showed that this is a distorted view of Christianity, which is consistently about the salvation of a people, the body of Christ. We are going together to God. Our joy and our hope are bound up with the progress of all on the way. The First Letter of John says, "We are writing this [to you] so that *our* joy may be complete" (1:4, emphasis added).

But what about a monastery? Doesn't it fit the critique of Christianity cited by the pope: "a way of abandoning the world to its misery and taking refuge in a private form of eternal salvation" (*Spe Salvi*, 13)? This is certainly the way religious life has often been considered, especially since the time of the Enlightenment. The French Revolution and other secularist movements into the twentieth century banned religious orders that had no observable use to the society. Some groups that served in hospitals and schools survived, but contemplative religious were the first to be eliminated.

The utilitarian norm is not wrong in itself: what we do must be good for something in this world. But there are other measures besides the materialistic. When the early monk Pachomius was asked why he was going away to the desert, he replied, "I am becoming a monk to save the world." This may sound grandiose, but it is to the point. Pachomius' remark reflects a sense of the interconnectedness of the divine and the human, and of time and eternity. The monk connects with God for the good of all. Bringing one life into order with God affects the whole.

Geologists tell us that an earthquake may be caused by something as small as the displacement of a sliver of rock deep within the earth. As the surrounding earth adjusts to this change, the reverberations become larger and larger until they erupt in an earthquake. In the same way, an individual life that is out of sync with sin can send a reverberation of grace into the world. It is what makes the life of a St. Thérèse of Lisieux, no matter how hidden or unknown, powerful for good at the time and forever afterward. In one of his poems, Cardinal John Henry Newman spoke of the hidden effect of even one Sign of the Cross:

> Whene'er across this sinful flesh of mine
>   I draw the Holy Sign,
> All good thoughts stir within me, and renew
>   Their slumbering strength divine;
>
> And who shall say, but hateful spirits around,
>   For their brief hour unbound,
> Shudder to see, and wail their overthrow?
>   While on far heathen ground
> Some lonely Saint hails the fresh odor, though
>   Its source he cannot know.
> ("The Sign of the Cross")

The monastic instinct flows from a conviction in the heart of Christianity that through the indwelling presence of God, a person of faith is potentially in touch with the whole world; and that by making oneself available in the humble obedience of prayer, a channel is opened for God's grace to flow to any or every need, whether known or not. Therefore, the authentic search for God anywhere, in a busy family life or in the silence of the cloister, is never selfish or individualistic. It is always seeking the good of the other. The combination of personal and communal in even the most secret prayer is put very beautifully by the monastic author of *The Cloud of Unknowing* in the late fourteenth century: "I tell you this, one loving blind desire for God alone is more valuable in itself, more pleasing to God and to the saints, more beneficial to your own growth, and more helpful to your friends, both living and dead, than anything else you could do" (9).

We respond where we are called. Sometimes this is to a very busy and hands-on service of others, and sometimes it is to a very secret search for God in silence. But always a true Christian vocation reaches out to others in love.

22. GOD AND SQUARE PEGS

The idiomatic expression "a square peg in a round hole" is a familiar way of describing the feeling of being out of place or ill at ease in an assignment that doesn't fit one's capabilities. Being put in such an awkward situation can cause frustration and even anger if it was imposed against our own better judgment. More careful planning could have avoided the mistake and the discomfort.

But when we review the history of God's choices and decisions for the working out of his plan of salvation, we notice that he seems to have a habit of calling people to important roles they feel ill prepared for and incompetent to carry out—square pegs for round holes.

The prime example is Moses, who was chosen for the key assignment of leading the Israelite people out of slavery in Egypt, an event that would be so pivotal in the drama of salvation. He protested immediately: "Who am I that I should go to Pharaoh and lead the Israelites out of Egypt?" (Exodus 3:11). He pointed out that he didn't even know God's name, and besides, he didn't have the speaking ability that a spokesman would need. He may also have thought about his age (by biblical reckoning, eighty years old), his criminal record in Egypt, and his outsider status after many years in exile.

Gideon was beating out wheat when the angel of the Lord appeared and told him he was chosen to save his people from the power of Midian. "Please, my lord," he answered, "how can I save Israel? My family is the meanest in Manasseh, and I am the most insignificant in my father's house" (Judges 6:15).

Amos was shepherding his flock when he was called, with no previous connection with prophets nor any idea of becoming a prophet himself (Amos 7:14). Jeremiah, like Moses, protested that he was not a speaker, and added, "I am too young" (Jeremiah 1:6).

Paul talked of himself as "born abnormally" to his role as an apostle, and said he was not fit to be called an apostle, "because I persecuted the church of God" (1 Corinthians 15:8-9).

Today it is a common hiring practice to create a job description and then conduct a search to find the right person to fit the need—a round peg for a round hole. Compared to this practice, God's way seems haphazard. Surely there were people better qualified by native ability and experience, not to mention eagerness, for the prophetic roles we have just described, and God would have known who they were.

A key to understanding God's reasoning is found in the story of Gideon. Gideon accepted the call to save the Israelites from Midian and went to work gathering an army from Manessah and other tribes until he had twenty-two thousand men. To his surprise, God told him he had too many soldiers. Why? Because when the army was victorious, Israel would say, "My own power brought me the victory" (Judges 7:2). God wanted the people to know without a doubt by whose power they were saved, so he had Gideon reduce his troops to three hundred.

In the same way, Paul said that though he knew he was unqualified on his own to be an apostle, "By the grace of God I am what I am" (1 Corinthians 15:10). Some of the Corinthians had pointed out his unworthiness; Paul didn't defend himself but said he would even boast of his weakness "in order that the power of Christ may dwell with me" (2 Corinthians 12:9).

There is nothing wrong with efficiency, but God can sacrifice efficiency for higher goals. He wants to offer the opportunity for us to put our trust in him with the kind of complete dependence that is the requirement for saving faith. As long as we are confident of our own resources, and as long as we have all our ducks in a row, it's hard to give up control. And as long as we are in control, God isn't needed. We can take care of ourselves.

St. Benedict has a chapter in his *Rule* on what a brother is to do when the abbot assigns him a task that he feels is impossible. The monk is not told simply to be quiet about his feelings and obey. He is given the opportunity to make his case (like Moses and the others) about why this assignment is not a good idea. The abbot may change his mind, but if he doesn't, says St. Benedict, "Trusting in God's help, [the brother] must in love obey" (*Rule of Benedict*, 68:5).

God is known to choose square pegs for round holes, and he can make them fit, but his main concern is helping us learn to trust him so that we can live with him and do his work.

23. THE RICH MAN

The gospel story of the rich man is a puzzler (Mark 10:17-22). Why does Jesus say that this man, who has been keeping the commandments since childhood, cannot be saved unless he sells his possessions and gives the money to the poor? Why does he have to do this when others don't?

Zacchaeus was praised for giving only half of his possessions away (Luke 19:8-10). Other well-to-do people, like Joseph of Arimathea (Mark 15:43) and the women who supported Jesus (Luke 8:3), apparently didn't have to do even that much. And then Jesus said those words that always make people squirm in their pews: "It is easier for a camel to pass through the eye of a needle than for one who is rich to enter the kingdom of God" (Mark 10:25).

The New Testament never says that riches are evil. Dangerous maybe, but not evil. In the hands of good people, wealth can be a blessing for themselves and many others. Sometimes the Bible is quoted as saying, "Money is the root of all evil." But this is a misreading of 1 Timothy 6:10, which says, "The *love* of money is the root of all evils." The Greek word is *philarguria*, the love of silver. It is not money but being consumed by the desire for it that creates the danger. Money itself is good and necessary.

An important clue to the interpretation of the story of the rich man is given in the passage that immediately precedes it, in which Jesus says, "Whoever does not accept the kingdom of God like a child will not enter it" (Mark 10:15). This doesn't mean one has to give up everything one has learned as an adult and be naïve or unquestioning. It means we must recognize our dependence on God and stop trying to control and manipulate everything in our lives. A child may be good or bad, clever or slow, but a child always knows that someone else is taking care of things.

Having an attitude of dependence on God is hard for the wealthy, because riches give power, and power feeds an illusion of control over one's destiny. Maybe I can build my own security without thinking about God. To be rich and dependent on God at the same time, on the other hand, is a wonderful thing, a source of great good in the world.

The Church has wrestled with the Bible story of the rich man from the earliest days. Widely quoted and copied since the third century was Clement of Alexandria's essay, "Who Is the Rich Man That Shall Be Saved?" "There is nothing great or enviable about having no money," he said. "If no one had anything, what opportunity would there be for sharing one's goods?" What we must banish from the heart is "attachment to money, excessive desire for it, morbid excitement over it, and anxiety about it" (XI, XIII).

Jesus could tell that the man in the story was not free within the gift of his riches, but that his possessions were keeping him enslaved. The man's response about having kept the commandments told Jesus that he considered his salvation assured because of his good observance. It was like anything else in his life: since he could buy anything that he wanted, he thought he could buy heaven too. Jesus saw that this particular person would not have a chance without breaking dramatically with his possessions, which were actually possessing him.

Money and material possessions are not the only kind of wealth. Our natural gifts and talents make us rich, as do the education and experience that have come our way. This kind of wealth can be life-giving, or like any riches, it may come between us and God. Properly used and appreciated, all riches are gifts of God that can bring us closer to him as grateful children and provide us with an abundance to use in service to others.

24. HOSPITALITY

In June 2002, a gunman entered Conception Abbey in Missouri and killed two monks before killing himself. The man had no known connection to the abbey or any of its monks. No motive has yet been discovered.

St. Benedict instructed his monks to receive all guests as Christ, "for he will say, 'I was a stranger and you welcomed me'" (*Rule of Benedict*, 53:1; Matthew 25:35). This application of Jesus' words has had a notable impact in inspiring Benedictine hospitality since then. Benedict did not originate this practice of monastic spirituality, which has always been a part of the monastic vocation, but his emphasis on the guest as Christ gave a powerful focus to the practice.

Benedict's own era was not a good time for open hospitality. He was born four years after the traditional date of the fall of the Roman Empire (A.D. 476). Institutions had broken down and the roads were not safe. Though many of the visitors to monasteries were pilgrims, you never knew who might show up at the door. Given the suspicious attitude toward guests in the *Rule of the Master*, written anonymously several decades before Benedict's and the main source for his own rule, we would not expect Benedict to adopt such a generous welcoming policy. Chapter 53 does build in some screening through prayer and conversation, but only after the guest is inside. It is a dangerous way to live, as the tragedy at Conception Abbey has illustrated dramatically.

It is, however, the gospel way. Until we have further information that might modify our judgment, the guest is to be received as good. We trust God to be present and to make things work out. The basic stance is open, trusting, and defenseless. Welcome— then ask questions. The stranger is immediately transformed into a guest. Accepting without judgment: this is surely a reason that Benedictine monasteries are favorite locations for ecumenical encounters and retreats. The way of the world is the opposite: judge first, then decide whether or not to allow entrance. Our unredeemed tendency is to be suspicious and to see the stranger as a threat, to give people entry only when they've earned it. We live mentally in a gated community.

Benedictine hospitality goes further than welcoming the stranger at the door. It is an attitude of welcome to everyone we meet, whether the first or second or thousandth time. Even within the community or family, time after time we are strangers to one another asking for entrance. In faith we must always make the stranger a guest. Our ongoing interactions are informed by our knowledge of one another and by judgments based on experience, but still we must be open to a new revelation of the person every time.

This is part of what it means to be a little child. "Unless you turn and become like children, you will not enter the kingdom of heaven" (Matthew 18:3). A child is dependent and defenseless and therefore trusts others to take care of security. A child wakes up to a new world everyday and can give everyone a new opportunity. But he will soon learn, as he begins to grow toward adulthood, how to hold grudges and prejudices.

In chapter 72 on "The Good Zeal of Monks," which is considered a synthesis of the rule's teaching, Benedict applies the doctrine of hospitality to life within the monastery by quoting St.

Paul to the Romans: "They should each try to be the first to show respect to the other" (*Rule of Benedict,* 72:4; Romans 12:10). The English word "respect" comes from the Latin and means literally to "look back," "look again." Often our first look is dimmed by prejudice and we cannot see the other person clearly. We need to take another look. The stranger looks like an interruption, a bother, a problem, maybe even a criminal. Look again: the stranger is Christ.

The Jewish Hasidim tell of the rabbi who asked his students, "How can you tell that night has ended and the day is coming?" A student answered, "When you can see clearly that an animal in the distance is a lion and not a leopard." "No," said the rabbi. "It is when you can recognize the stranger as your sister or brother. Until you are able to do so, it is still night."

25. THE GIFT OF SILENCE

There is a great hunger for silence in our time. We notice it in the monastery, where people come simply looking for an oasis of stillness. It isn't only the outer noise, though there is plenty of that, with computers and cell phones and radios and TVs. These media serve greatly to enhance movement and communication, but they also expose us instantaneously to the news of every tragedy, scandal, and disaster in the world, so that even when there is no sound, the inner noise is deafening.

We desire to turn the volume down not only outside but inside—to be enveloped by silence. The model of silence in Scripture and the Church is Mary, who fixed a contemplative gaze on her son and "pondered all these things in her heart" (see Luke 2:51). The favorite images of Mary in art are the moments of silence: the annunciation; the scene at the crib—as a Christmas carol says, "How silently, how silently, the wondrous gift is given"; and Mary holding the body of Jesus in her arms beneath the cross. The silence of Mary is not an empty silence. It is a silence of contemplation: of waiting, of pondering, of loving. Mary pondering the message of Gabriel at the beginning and Mary with Jesus at the end: these are two different moments—of bewilderment, surprise, and apprehension, and of loss, pain, and sorrow. The word that comes out of these moments is then and for all eternity the word of acceptance, submission: *Fiat*, "let it be."

Every day in the monastery begins in this contemplative silence. Monks have the luxury of rising only for the purpose of praising God. We do not have to clothe children or hurry out to a job in town. Our first words of the day are "O Lord, open my lips." After the silence of the night, we present ourselves to God before moving back into the daily activity, asking God to guide us in using the gift of speech through the day: "O Lord, open my lips, and let my mouth proclaim your praise." In the modern world, it may seem as if silence interrupts the flow of our lives, but the truth is we are surrounded by an ocean of divine silence. We do not leave our work to enter silence, but we leave silence to enter our work.

But silence comes in many forms. There is charitable silence, when we keep something harmful or hateful to ourselves; the silence of awe in the presence of great beauty; and the silence of peace. In prayer we open ourselves to contemplative silence before the face of God. There is the silence of keeping a confidence, the silence of patient waiting, the silence of sharing another's suffering. But there are also the negative and hostile silences: the silence of smoldering anger, the silence of sitting in judgment, the silence of fear. There is the cowardly silence that prevents us from speaking against injustice, and the selfish silence in which I hoard my time and my person for myself. There is the so-called "silent treatment," by which I make someone pay for having offended me.

Obviously, true silence isn't the same as the lack of sound. In the false and punishing kinds of silence, there is turmoil inside, deafening noise, maybe even a volcano. If you say the wrong word to a person, there may be an explosion. You say something you think is innocent and touch a raw nerve. There cannot be silence until the inner wound is healed.

True silence permeates a person. There is peace inside even when there is conflict outside. Such peace is a gift we can only prepare for, not create. But it is a gift God wants to give us. We open our hearts and wait confidently in silence and faith and prayer.

26. Fear of the Lord (and Nobody Else)

The Bible tells us that "The fear of the Lord is the beginning of wisdom" (Psalm 111:10). For most of us, this is a very hard saying. Fear of the Lord is the very thing that has caused so much trouble. For some, it inspires a religious observance of servility and dread. Others find it impossible to believe in a God who is so tyrannical. We are happy for the liberation that has come with the understanding that the God revealed in the Bible is a God of love, not of fear. We don't want to return to a fearful religion. The experience of many has been that the fear of the Lord is not the beginning but the end of wisdom.

Obviously something is wrong here. To live in fear, in the ordinary sense, is a very bad thing and the source of enormous human misery. But there is another sense, the sense of the biblical statement, in which living in fear is an inevitable part of the human condition. If correctly understood and accepted, it becomes the source of joy, peace, and happiness. To live in fear in this sense is to realize who or what is the master of one's existence, and then to accept this mastery and live according to its demands. There is only one who can live without this kind of fear: God.

St. Paul saw clearly that because we cannot be our own masters, we are going to serve either God, the true master who offers life, or Satan, the deceiver who offers death. "But what profit did you get then from the things of which you are now ashamed? For the end of those things is death. But now that you have been freed from sin and have become slaves of God, the benefit that you have leads to sanctification, and its end is eternal life" (Romans 6:21-22).

We cringe at the word "slave," even slave of God, which is understandable because of our national history. "Servant" is just as good, as long as we mean by it absolute subservience and obedience to God as the master of our existence. There is no other way to human liberation. Anything short of it is a trap.

If we think about it, we can see that in everything we do, all day long, moment by moment, we are expressing obedience to some master. If you let me lead you to sin, in that moment I am your master, and you fear me more than God. Whenever you or I depart from doing God's will as we understand it, in that moment we are fearing another master, whether it is a companion, a cinema or sports idol, the government, a business system, or a passion. We have bound ourselves to a master who has no power to do good for us, only harm. And most of the time, we have not identified the master, which makes the slavery blind.

What if I am afraid to confront you about something serious because of what you might say? As long as that binds me, I fear you and I am your slave. What if I am afraid to be myself, to live for the values I espouse? Someone has enslaved me in fear, and it is not God.

To be a free human being, I must know at every moment who my master is, and I must choose to serve. My master can only be either God or evil in one of its myriad disguises, because I am not my own master, and there is no master in between God and evil. There is no "demilitarized zone," no neutral country.

Only God has my best interests at heart, knows what is best for me in every moment, and loves me. God lets me be myself, with no masks. That, and only that, is true freedom. "The fear of the LORD is the beginning of wisdom."

27. Hoping for a Better Past

A bishop told a story about himself at an anniversary celebration some years ago. He said that when he received the call from the apostolic delegate informing him that he had been appointed a bishop, he was also sworn to secrecy until the announcement could be made a few weeks later.

It was hard to think of anything else during the next few days as he went about his work, knowing that arrangements were going to have to be made to cover a multitude of obligations already lined up for him. Most of all, he was burning to tell his co-workers and members of his family, especially his mother.

On the day of the announcement, he was finally permitted to alert those close to him, so the first person he called was his mother. "Mother," he said, trying to sound matter-of-fact, "there is going to be an announcement on TV today that I have been appointed a bishop." His mother responded, "I told your father when you were a little boy that we should have had your teeth straightened."

This deflating response was not what he had been expecting. It brought him back to reality, and later he was able to appreciate it and laugh about it. But there was something else going on in his mother's response that relates to what this chapter is about. His announcement triggered in her a regret about the past, maybe a wry regret, that something that could have been done was not done. In other words, she was hoping for a better past.

As soon as we hear her regret phrased this way, we recognize that "hoping for a better past" is a waste of time. The past is the past, and it won't come back. But our lives may be tinged by this hopeless desire every day without our being aware of it. We find our thoughts going back again and again to what might have been: what if I had finished college, what if I had taken that job, what if I had not married so young, what if I had become a missionary sister. A certain wistfulness (like the statement of the bishop's mother) is certainly not harmful, but an overindulgence in this sort of thing can fuel depression or a life of anger and sadness. Then, it isn't only about the distant past but about what I shouldn't have done or said this morning, and I am never at peace.

This is not the same as reasonable regret for misdeeds, and certainly not the same as compunction, in which our sins of the past become a stimulus for conversion. It is rather about stewing over events of the past that are matters of history and can never be changed. Sooner or later we branch out from reconstructing our own past lives into reconstructing the lives of others and even the larger history of the state or the Church, and we bore others with our fantasy of how things would be better now "if only" things had gone differently in the past. We become angry over and over again with figures of the past long dead, in the larger history or in our own life.

It is important to study and analyze the past, and even our own past, in order to learn how to live in the present and future. The past is a very important teacher. But we must live in the present moment, not in the past. Fr. Jean Pierre de Caussade, a spiritual writer of the eighteenth century, has taught us to speak of the "sacrament of the present moment."

The spiritual condition that is the antidote to and the opposite of brooding about what might have been is acceptance.

Acceptance is a spiritual attitude based on trust in the provident mercy of God. It is captured by St. Paul's statement: "We know that all things work for good for those who love God, who are called according to his purpose" (Romans 8:28). This doesn't mean that everything that happens is pleasing or beneficial in the way I want. What pleases me may not seem good to someone else. Acceptance starts with an awareness that reality does not adapt itself to me, and that this is a good thing. I must adapt myself to reality, which seen with the eyes of faith is Reality—God himself.

Acceptance does not look mainly at the past. It only takes one look backward in order to accept what has been. Acceptance is an attitude of looking forward, of facing life as it comes, of being ready to receive, as a gift of God, whatever comes along. With God's grace we do the best we can in responding to the people and events of every day, and if we say the wrong thing or have a misunderstanding or misinterpret how we should deal with someone, we admit it, examine what went wrong, and ask for forgiveness if we have been at fault. But we do not keep looking back at what happened, or pick it up and carry it around our necks. We leave it behind and go forward, trusting God's love and providence as life unfolds before us.

Part V

The End
and Beyond

28. THE WORK GOES ON

The monks living in the infirmary are regularly referred to as "retired monks." We know what this means: they are no longer involved in the day-to-day work of the monastery. This is an adjustment to the workplace mentality of the surrounding society, in which to be retired means to leave the work that has been one's main source of livelihood and a major concentration of energy and interest. In our consumer society, it may mean that one is no longer considered important and is viewed as having no contribution to make.

But in an important sense, "retired monks" is an oxymoron, because monks never retire from their main work, which is a life of intercession for the world.

In some ways the main work of a monk intensifies when physical limitations break in. Some of our most active intercessors—in a sense those on the front lines in our mission for the Church—are those restricted by age and infirmity. The ordinary work of this world (of which monks have plenty) comes to an end for each of us, but the work of faithful intercession goes on. It is not stopped by any disease or even by death.

This "post-work work" is not limited to monks. Every retired person may take heart that there is still a focus for life and still much to do. But it is inside work, work inside the person, where one may lay down one's life as a channel of grace for the world. God could certainly do everything without us, but through the incarnation, he has called for our help. A person sidelined from activity by age or infirmity may say with St. Paul: "I rejoice in my sufferings for your sake, and in my flesh I am filling up what is lacking in the afflictions of Christ on behalf of his body, which is the church" (Colossians 1:24).

Sometimes a monk may become mentally impaired by senility or Alzheimer's disease, and may even completely lose rational control. The work of intercession goes on. This is because a life of intercession is something gradually built up by many daily decisions and prayers over the years and is eventually not subject to accidental change. A pattern of fidelity grows into a habitual decision for God and the kingdom based in the will. It becomes a habitual decision to serve God, which is not stopped by external forces or circumstances, even a psychologically or mentally debilitating illness.

When a person is no longer able to attend daily or even Sunday Mass, or is in a hospital or in a nursing home and is unable to read or maybe even think, participation in the work of Christ goes on. A fidelity that was built up in the active years remains constant. The decision for God is unbroken, and the intercession flowing from that faithful life continues to bless the world. Is it effective? The Church thinks so: St. Thérèse of Lisieux, who never left her monastery, has been named patron of missionary work alongside St. Francis Xavier, who spent his life in constant travel and hands-on ministry in India, Malaysia, and Japan.

29. A Joy to Be Around

Fr. Harold Heiman lived to be ninety-four years old. At the end he needed a wheelchair to get around and had many other limitations. Long ago he had been forced to give up driving because of failing eyesight. A once very active man and an avid golfer, he had to spend most of his time watching old movies on TV. Sometimes you could see that he was in pain, probably the residual effects of one or more of the seventeen surgeries he had undergone during his lifetime.

But in his presence, you were never struck by a sense of limitation or loss. He was always upbeat and optimistic, and his answer to "How are you doing?" or "How are you feeling?" was "Wonderful. I never had it so good." People not only loved him, they loved to be with him. It did him good, but it also did them good.

Everyone who lives long enough will be faced with accepting old age. We will have to let some new realities into our lives and let go of some things we've taken for granted, especially the gifts of health and mobility. Some handle this well and others do not. Though aging is part of the natural process of life and something to be observed in ourselves and in others every day, when it happens to us, it can catch us by surprise. Though old age comes naturally, accepting it well does not. Some grow into it with dignity and peace and even humor, and are a joy to be around, like Fr. Harold, while others cannot accept it and make other people pay, whether they mean to or not. Aging well takes a decision, an overall decision that then unfolds in small decisions throughout every day.

The diminishments that come with old age seem to strike some as a surprise, as a development they hadn't been expecting. They think it is unfair, or a mistake, or a problem that surely can be rectified once it is pointed out. This attitude is supported by our culture's assumption that anything can be fixed by medication, with the corollary that we deserve to have whatever it takes to fix the problem.

But, as a spiritual writer has pointed out, the diminishments of age do not surprise God. That's the way he built us. God would be surprised if we didn't experience the curtailments of our health and strength as we near the end of our time on earth. Our life is an arc of ascent and descent. And this is for our good, because the project of this life is to learn how to turn over control to the Creator so that we may have the interior freedom to leave this world in peace and be ready for new life with God. If we haven't been able to surrender before our body begins breaking down, the gradual reduction of our abilities gives us a new opportunity before we die; if we have begun to surrender, the suffering and diminishment give us an opportunity for even deeper freedom from ego and self. We all have to die, but we have a choice whether to give our life or have it wrenched from us.

For the most part, we deal with aging with the pattern we have already set for dealing with life. By God's grace, some people experience a conversion as old age begins to take its toll, and change from demanding to accepting, from griping and accusing and projecting frustration on their caregivers to accepting their care with gratitude. But that is a rare gift. More typically, those who have been demanding before will continue to be unable to yield to life in old age.

This is not a problem of temperament but a spiritual issue. St. Benedict warned the monks against murmuring, which is not occasional griping but a deadly attitude of complaint that betrays a lack of trust in God in the day-to-day of life. Maybe God isn't present, or doesn't care, or maybe he is unable to do anything. When the Israelites became thirsty in the desert, they didn't merely cry out in distress. They doubted God's care: "Is the LORD in our midst or not?" (Exodus 17:7). One's trust or lack of trust in God is revealed in the crucible of old age. When the issue of acceptance is still unresolved, this struggle creates a purgatory for the angry patient and everyone involved, but when acceptance has been achieved with the inner freedom and peace it brings, the elderly person is blessed and becomes for everyone a joy to be around. ⤬

30. A CLOUD OF WITNESSES

I like to go down to our monastic cemetery and stroll reflectively as I read the names of the monks who are buried under the tombstones. By now I have known about half of the nearly 150 members of our community who have died since our founding in 1878. My stroll is a reminiscence but also a communion. These men are still members of our community and a presence among us. For them, "life is changed, not ended" (Preface for Christian Death I, *Roman Missal*), and the same is true of our relationship with them. I don't walk among the graves as in a picture gallery or a museum, reviving my memories of the past. I commune with the monks identified by their tombstones, who are not there in the flesh but are still alive.

The Letter to the Hebrews says we are surrounded by "so great a cloud of witnesses" as we follow Jesus, "the leader and perfecter of faith" (12:1, 2). The author has just finished presenting a long list of witnesses, stretching back to Abel, who have gone ahead of us but are still with us. Since the time of the writing of Hebrews, of course, the cloud has increased monumentally. Every year more people who have died in faith are added to the group, not to speak of the faithful believers who are alive with us during our time.

All of these people, dead or alive, help us on the journey, and we help them. We are more conscious of depending on and relating to the people alive with us in our earthly walk, especially our family and close friends. That is wonderful, but it is not enough, and in creating us, God knew it would not be enough for us. We are not orphans in time, isolated from the other generations who lived at other times. It is not enough to have the examples of the great believers of the past, the prophets and the apostles, the virgins and confessors, as helpful as that is. We need their presence, and by a great blessing of God, we have it. A hymn in the Common for Holy Men and Women in the Liturgy of the Hours expresses it beautifully:

> May all that splendid company
> Whom Christ our Savior came to meet
> Help us on our uneven road
> Made smoother by their passing feet.

We call this reality of eternal relationship the Communion of Saints, describing it in terms of the Church Militant, those who are alive now; the Church Suffering, those who have died faithful to God but are receiving their purification for final union; and the Church Triumphant, those who are already enjoying God's presence completely in heaven. What a wonderful doctrine, something unique to Christians among all who have a belief in God. But I'm not sure we take full advantage of it.

Within the great cloud of witnesses that reaches back through all the generations, each of us has a cloud of witnesses that God has provided particularly for us. We are conscious of the support of many faithful people as we make our journey to the kingdom: our parents and family, relatives, teachers, priests and religious, mentors, and special friends. We lean on them, we ask their prayers, and we try to support them too. When they precede us in death, we pray for them. But do we pray to them? We pray to the canonized saints, but do we pray to those who are not canonized but who we know are in the presence of God, in purgatory if not yet heaven? We prayed to them (asked for their prayers) while they were alive; why not now when they are secure forever in their relationship with God?

When an infant is desperately sick or a teenager is reeling in adolescent chaos, why not call on someone close to you for help, who had to deal with such problems years ago, but who now has gone before you in the sign of faith? Or why not someone who overcame a difficult adolescence? If in business there are issues with personnel or with finances, why not turn for help to a friend among your cloud of witnesses who also struggled with such problems?

I find it very helpful when walking among my departed brothers in the cemetery to ask particular ones for help in areas in which they were involved, or to thank them for continuing to walk with me and the community as we follow them and build on the foundation they laid. I certainly pray to the abbots, who were standing where I am now. I even pray to people who lived on our property long before us, especially the Native Americans whose artifacts tell us they have been on this land since thousands of years before Christ. Many of them are saints because of their fidelity to the divine call as it came to them. I appeal to them when we have questions about developing the property or what to plant where, because they cared about this land long before we did, and we are still in it together.

What a marvel it would be if suddenly the veil fell away and we could see the cloud of witnesses surrounding us. What a source of comfort and hope that would be. But whether we can see them or not, the witnesses are with us, though for the present we can see them only with the eyes of faith. ⬯⬯

Sources

Selections from Pope Benedict XVI's encyclicals *God Is Love* and *Spe Salvi* accessed at vatican.va.

Selections from John Henry Newman's *Parochial and Plain Sermons* accessed at newmanreader.org.

George Herbert's poem "Love" accessed at poetry-archive.com.

Selections from the *Rule of Benedict* are taken from *The Rule of Benedict in English*, edited by Timothy Fry, The Liturgical Press, Collegeville, Minnesota, 1982. On the Web at christdesert.org.

Selections from *The Cloud of Unknowing* taken from *The Cloud of Unknowing and the Book of Privy Counseling*, edited by William Johnston, Doubleday Image, New York, 1973.

Selection from St. John Climacus taken from *The Ladder of Divine Ascent*, Classics of Western Spirituality, Paulist Press, Mahwah, New Jersey, 1982.

Selection from the Institutes by John Cassian taken from *The Nicene and Post-Nicene Fathers*, Second Series, E.C.S. Gibson, Vol. 11. William Eerdmans, Grand Rapids, Michigan, 1964.

Selection from St. Francis de Sales taken from feastofsaints.com /fdes.htm.

John Henry Newman's poem "The Sign of the Cross" accessed at poemhunter.com.

Selection from Clement of Alexandria taken from *The Ante-Nicene Fathers*, Vol. II, translated by William Wilson, Charles Scribner's Sons, New York, 1926.

Selection from the Liturgy of the Hours, Hymn for the Common of Holy Men and Women, found at adoremus.org/0307LiturgyofHours.html.